Equality Stories
recognition, respect and raising achievement

Equality Stories

recognition, respect and raising achievement

Robin Richardson and Berenice Miles

SCHOOLS AND LOCAL EDUCATION AUTHORITIES IN MULTI-ETHNIC BRITAIN

tb

Trentham Books

Stoke on Trent, UK and Sterling, USA

Trentham Books Limited

Westview House	22883 Quicksilver Drive
734 London Road	Sterling
Oakhill	VA 20166-2012
Stoke on Trent	USA
Staffordshire	
England ST4 5NP	

First published 2003
reprinted 2004

British Library Cataloguing-in-Publication Data
A catalogue record for this book is available from the British Library

1 85856 266 X

Designed and typeset by Trentham Print Design Ltd., Chester and printed in Great Britain by Cromwell Press Ltd., Wiltshire.

Photographs by Rachel Malik

CONTENTS

EQUALITY

The local education authority featured in this book is real. It has been given a fictitious name, however, since its stories, aspirations and experiences are not unique.

DIVERSITY

COHESION

LIST OF BOXES

ACKNOWLEDGEMENTS

London Borough of Ealing

Acknowledgement is due to senior officers and inspectors in the London Borough of Ealing for the support and leadership which they gave to the projects and stories presented in this book. They include in particular Caroline Whalley, currently executive director and formerly director of the School Standards Division.

Steering committee

The members of the working party which initiated the projects in this book were David Baldwin, Veena Bedi, Morag Bowden, Roger Butler, Jane Gabb, Jas Grewal, Jas Kalra-Phull, Pauline Lyseight-Jones, Rosemary Matthews, Berenice Miles, Sandya Mohindra, Elaine Noden, Updesh Porter, Daphne Richards and Robin Richardson. Administrative and secretarial support was provided by Paul Fish, Shirley McDowell, Manjit Khera and Yvonne Tibbles.

Schools

The programme reported on in this book had three components: Inclusive Classrooms, Inclusive Schools; Inspirations, Aspirations; and Ealing Raising African-Caribbean Achievement in Schools (ERACAS). The schools involved in one or more of these three projects were Acton Early Years Education Centre, Acton High, Blair Peach Primary, Brentside High, Cardinal Wiseman RC High, Costons Primary, Dormers Wells High, Downe Manor Primary, Edward Betham CE Primary, Ellen Wilkinson School for Girls, Gifford Primary, Hambrough Primary, Horsenden Primary, Montpelier Primary, North Primary, Selborne Primary, Southall Early Years Education Centre, Southfield Primary, Three Bridges Primary, Tudor Primary and West Twyford Primary. Acknowledgement is due to all the headteachers and governing bodies, and to all colleagues who assisted or supported.

Individual teachers

The teachers who took an active part in one or more of the projects were Fatima Ali, Sharon Baker, Carmel Cameron, Chris Coakley, Fauzia Dualah, Sadia Edross, Saeda Elmi, Jawahir Farah, Navdeep Gill, Enya Glanz, Theresa Gleeson, Karin Gordon, Suzanne Goodwin, Anu Gray, Kam Grewal-Saini, Ros Hancell, Irene Hawke, Elaine Hood, Deborah Hope, Mandy Hudson, Janet Ingram, Carole Khunan, Vijay Kondel, Dominique Mann, Janet McHugh, Vivien Morris, Ingrid Muir, Elaine Noden, Mia Ospovat-Stockton, Ann O'Sullivan, Felicity Parry, Amy Pitcairn, Updesh Porter, Sioned Pughe, Katherine Ross, Jyoti Shah, Sheila Vizard, Elizabeth Walton and Kate Whelan.

Consultants

Consultants from outside Ealing assisted with the programme which gave rise to this book. They were Stella Dadzie, Jozimba Panthera, Elaine Mace, Brian Richardson, Stuart Scott, Caitlin Walker and Verna Wilkins.

Others

Acknowledgement is due to Gregory George, Buhle Miles and Alan Parker; to Lance Lewis and Kirklees Education Authority; and to the many pupils who are quoted directly or indirectly in the pages of this book.

Responsibility

Views expressed or implied in this book are the responsibility of the authors. They are not to be understood as necessarily reflecting official policy in the local authority from which the book derives, nor as representing the views of any of the individuals and schools mentioned above.

Key publications

The book draws throughout on the *Stephen Lawrence Inquiry report* (the Macpherson Report) and *The Future of Multi-Ethnic Britain* (the Parekh Report).

Issues in the Lawrence Inquiry report have been vividly introduced for children in *The Life of Stephen Lawrence* by Verna Allette Wilkins, published by Tamarind Books. It received its official launch at Ealing Town Hall on 24 March 2001, having previously been piloted in a number of Ealing schools.

Insted consultancy

Ealing commissioned Robin Richardson, a director of the Insted consultancy, to assist with the planning and organisation of the *Inclusive Classrooms, Inclusive Schools* project. Other Insted projects in recent years have included:

- Compilation of *Inclusive Schools, Inclusive Society* for the Association of London Government, Race On the Agenda and Save the Children, published by Trentham Books in 1999.

- Editing and consultancy for *The Future of Multi-Ethnic Britain*, Profile Books 2000.

- Compilation of materials for the Commission on British Muslims and Islamophobia, 1997-2002.

Photography

All photographs are by Rachel Malik.

Quotations and references

The sources of quotations and ideas are acknowledged on pages 89-90.

LOCAL LEADERSHIP AND SUPPORT

In February 2000 as Director of the School Standards Division I wrote to all headteachers in the borough inviting them to send two representatives to a conference in March. The title of that conference was 'Inclusive Classrooms, Inclusive Schools'. There was a tremendous response, and almost all our schools were represented, many by headteachers and governors. The conference was intended to develop new ways of using the Ethnic Minority Achievement Grant funding for professional and school development, since at this time there was more flexibility after the changeover from Section 11. The conference launched a programme of largely school-based development, planned by members of the Inspection and Advisory Service and headteachers and led by an external consultant.

Schools were given the opportunity to design and manage their own school-based projects focusing on priorities identified from the pupil data we collect from schools. The process has taught us all a lot about innovative ways of working. It sparked off imaginative ideas from schools and gave them the opportunity to put them into practice. Just as important it has put this professional development project firmly within the context of whole school development and given us a model we could adapt and use in other ways.

After the first year of the programme our EMAG funding for training was devolved to schools, and several schools took on the same model by creating special, time-limited projects to focus on particular issues. The leadership role of the Authority has been critical in supporting this initiative that has raised the profile of promoting equality in our schools and affirmed our commitment to continuing action on recommendations from the Stephen Lawrence Inquiry. The commitment of teachers and the support of headteachers have been impressive and they deserve our congratulations.

Caroline Whalley, Executive Director, Education and Lifelong Learning
London Borough of Ealing, October 2002

I This book's story
– background, aims and themes

Stories

'Stories,' Ben Okri has said, 'are the secret reservoir of values: change the stories individuals and nations live by and tell themselves and you change the individuals and nations.' He continues: 'Nations and peoples are largely the stories they feed themselves. If they tell themselves stories that are lies, they will suffer the future consequences of those lies. If they tell themselves stories that face their own truths, they will free their histories for future flowerings.'

This book contains, and it is itself contained by, stories. The stories it contains are to do with projects in schools and a local education authority, and with the three Rs in its sub-title – recognition, respect and raising achievement. The wider stories to which the book belongs are to do with the development of Britain as a multi-ethnic society, and with recent educational history. Ben Okri's points and reflections about story-telling in personal and national life, quoted above and in Box 1, set the scene for the book as a whole.

The origins of the book lie in one particular local education authority, referred to with the fictitious name 'Oakwell'. The real name of the authority is no secret, and can readily be seen in the list of acknowledgements. So why adopt the device of a fictitious name? There are several reasons. First, the projects reported on here took place against a background of influences, pressures and legal requirements which all local authorities have in common. The use of a fictitious name helps to emphasise that the authority is similar, so far as the national context is concerned, to all other authorities – it is not a special case.

Second, a fictitious name in the main body of the text helps to protect the anonymity of schools, teachers and pupils.

Third, the use of fictitious names helps to focus on the nature of story itself. The accounts in these pages are all true in the sense that important historical facts have not been altered or invented. But they are necessarily selective – some of their features are highlighted and foregrounded, and others are de-emphasised or omitted – and occasionally small details have been added to provide a fuller sense of context, or to ensure that a school or individual is not identifiable. The book is not fiction, but nor does it aim for the strict accuracy of academic research. The tone is closer to that of teachers

> Box 1
>
> ## The nature of stories
>
> Stories are as ubiquitous as water or air, and as essential. There is not a single person who is not touched by the silent presence of stories.
>
> Great leaders tell their nations fictions that alter their perceptions. Napoleon exemplified this, and made himself into an enthralling story. Even bad leaders know the power of negative stories.
>
> Alexander the Great conquered all of the known world. But Alexander himself was gently conquered by Homer.
>
> The fact of story-telling hints at a fundamental human unease, hints at human imperfection. Where there is perfection there is no story to tell.
>
> When we have made an experience or a chaos into a story we have transformed it, made sense of it, transmuted experience, domesticated the chaos.
>
> Homo fabula: we are story-telling beings.
>
> Stories are always a form of resistance.
>
> Source: *Birds of Heaven* by Ben Okri, Phoenix 1996

talking reflectively in their staffroom or at an inservice training session; and in certain respects the book is like a scrapbook or album, a miscellany of reminiscences, souvenirs, reminders and realia. The intention is to share experience, and through such sharing to reflect on it, and to invite comment and reflection from others. The book has been edited and formatted so that it can be used in inservice training.

In addition to stories from schools and inservice training events there are other kinds of story here as well. They include extracts from the writings and conversations of pupils, and from novels and autobiography. Further, there are reflections, explanations and commentary. These derive directly from involvement and interaction with lived stories – they are not mere think-pieces.

The book's pattern

In the next section of this first chapter there is an outline of how the story in Oakwell began and how it unfolded. Most of the projects reported on in the book were funded under the auspices of central government's Ethnic Minority Achievement Grant (EMAG). Accordingly there is an account of how Oakwell responded to EMAG, and of how it exploited the new opportunities which EMAG opened up. Other authorities have responded in broadly similar ways. The chapter ends by commenting on the concept of equality in the book's title, and stresses that two further values are also essential.

Chapter 2 is about the theory and practice of professional development. Entitled 'How workshops work', it contains several of the discussion exercises and materials that were developed and used at the courses, workshops and conferences in Oakwell, and explains the rationale behind them. There are also many cross-references to later chapters, for these too contain training materials.

Chapter 3, 'Listening, welcome and inclusion', describes how seven schools responded in their own situations to the overall Oakwell programme. The stories include a survey of opinions conducted amongst refugee and asylum-seeking pupils; accounts of work with Somali pupils and parents; and work with children who are new to English.

Chapter 4, 'Great expectations', draws together threads from the stories in the previous chapter and includes a further story from an Oakwell school. It recalls research findings over the years that pupils' achievements are greatly affected by what teachers and schools expect. The research is easier described than acted on, however. Complex and sensitive issues of social class, ethnicity and race are involved, and of adult/child and adult/adolescent relationships. Further, conventional notions relating to IQ and so-called ability have to be critically examined. Theories of multiple intelligence, preferred learning style and accelerated learning appear promising, but only if they are applied in an explicitly antiracist framework, as in the Oakwell school with which the chapter begins.

Chapter 5, 'We all have a story to tell', starts with a description of a project celebrating shared aspirations and cultural differences in one particular Oakwell neighbourhood. It opens then naturally to a discussion of the national picture, and of conflicting views of national history and identity. It cites the argument of the Commission on the Future of Multi-Ethnic Britain that Britain should be pictured as 'a community of communities' – not only in the present and future but also in the past – and considers the implications of this idea for citizenship education and personal and social education. A fundamental question in all citizenship education, it says, is 'What happens when people disagree?'

Chapter 6, 'Dealing with racisms', outlines key ideas and concepts – the distinction between colour racism and cultural racism, for example, and between institutional racism and personal – and discusses three main tasks for schools: preventing and addressing racist incidents; teaching about race and racism, and about equality and justice; and tackling institutional racism in school structures and organisation. The chapter includes a model school policy for race equality. This reflects the requirements of the Race Relations Amendment Act but also includes components that are logically necessary, over and above the strict legal requirements, if school policies are to be effective. The chapter closes with thoughts by pupils about the story of Stephen Lawrence. These are an appropriate end not only for the chapter but for the book as whole.

Notes and references in Chapter 7 include the sources of quotations in the main text, addresses of useful websites, suggestions for further reading, and a select bibliography.

School-based professional development

The influences on schools relevant to this book include the Stephen Lawrence Inquiry report, the Ofsted framework for inspecting inclusion, the requirements and expectations associated with the Ethnic Minority Achievement Grant (EMAG), the Race Relations Amendment Act 2000 and major national reports such as *The Future of Multi-Ethnic Britain*. They were mediated in Oakwell by an EMAG professional development group linked to the Education Department's equalities working party. Members of these two groups included headteachers, parents, community representatives, inspectors and officers.

When the EMAG was first introduced, it was resolved that funding for professional development should be retained centrally, but that it should be fully tied in with a grants system for practical projects in schools. Accordingly, all schools entitled to EMAG funding were invited to submit proposals. Part of the invitation is shown in Box 2. The grants were not large – only £1,500 each – but it was hoped and expected that they would act as catalysts for significant change. As an overall title for the project the working party chose the phrase Inclusive Classrooms, Inclusive Schools.

Schools were given broad guidelines about what would and would not be eligible. It was stressed that projects had to be about the professional development of staff within the overall framework of raising achievement, and that particular consideration would be paid to projects focusing on African-Caribbean achievement; literacy and numeracy; monitoring; and addressing institutional racism.

There were three further preliminary conditions:

- Schools would have to send two delegates, one of whom should be the headteacher or deputy head, to the project's inaugural one-day conference

- Schools should send at least one delegate to a 24-hour residential workshop to be held ten days after the conference

- Schools should be ready to share their experience with others, and to invite comment.

In due course 22 applications were accepted. Since some involved two or more schools working together, about a third of all schools in Oakwell were involved, and more than half of the schools in Oakwell entitled to substantial EMAG funding. A handful of applications were turned down because they did not meet the criterion stressing professional development. In a few instances applications were slightly re-negotiated in conversations between the headteacher and the LEA officer responsible for the scheme as a whole.

Box 2

How it all began

Inclusive Classrooms, Inclusive Schools
Invitation to apply for support for small school-based projects

CRITERIA FOR APPLICATION FOR SUPPORT

☐ Projects must relate to the principles of the Ethnic Minority Achievement Grant, to raise achievement of black, ethnic minority and refugee pupils

☐ Projects must relate to teacher development

☐ Schools must be willing to share results of the project with colleagues

When choosing which projects to support, we hope and intend that the final selection will include most or all of the following range:

☐ projects linked to achievement of pupils of African-Caribbean heritage

☐ projects linked to literacy

☐ projects linked to numeracy

☐ projects linked to monitoring

☐ projects linked to addressing institutional racism, as recommended in the Stephen Lawrence Inquiry

This is a staff and school development project and the expectation is that at least 80 per cent of the funding will be spent on supply cover or consultancy. A brief outline of your proposal should be submitted on one page of A4.

Inaugural conference

At the inaugural one-day conference at Oakwell Town Hall, opened by the chief education officer, there were some 120 participants. They reflected between them a wide range of perspective and seniority – there were bilingual classroom assistants, headteachers, grant-funded and mainstream teachers, elected members, LEA officers, inspectors and school governors. The range of status and experience was much commented on in the evaluation forms filled in at the end of the day. The morning programme consisted of a keynote lecture about the implications for schools of the Stephen Lawrence Inquiry report, followed by structured discussion activities in small groups. Some of the materials used in these activities appear later in this book.

In the afternoon the conference broke into committees of inquiry, each chaired jointly by a headteacher and a member of the LEA inspection and advisory service. They were held in the Council's committee rooms, hence in a context of weight and seriousness, though not undue solemnity. Within each committee every school participating in the programme was requested to explain what it was doing or proposing to do with its grant. Enabling questions were asked, and supportive words of advice and caveat were offered, by other people present. This built a strong sense of peer accountability – headteachers felt accountable to their colleagues in other schools rather than, or as well as, the local authority and central government.

At the end of the day participants were invited to jot notes about their feelings and reflections. 'Positive atmosphere – inspires change and is very motivating,' wrote someone. There are further extracts from the jottings in Box 3.

Residential workshops

A week or so after the inaugural conference there was a 24-hour residential workshop for about 30 participants. The first day was structured around discussion activities exploring issues of personal, professional and cultural identity, and the nature, history and dynamics of racism. Some of the papers appear in this book. The second day involved substantial discussion in small groups about the various school-based projects which had all by now made further progress. Again, a purpose was to

---

Box 3

'Can't wait to tell everyone' – reflections at the inaugural conference

'Very positive – for the first time to see people of all cultures, all roles, all levels – teachers, headteachers people from the authority – working purposefully together on a single task – especially since the task was eliminating racism!'

'A melting pot of people, ideas, realities and new possibilities, very exciting.'

'The conference has lifted our spirits and finally we will be heard. Racism will be out.'

'I hope that the shooting star of this conference is carried across the skies for infinity and does not fizzle out too far.'

'Nostalgic and heartening, to be discussing race issues explicitly again. And a great help in charting a way forward.'

'An amazing opportunity to meet people with a seemingly endless amount of knowledge and advice. I wasn't sure I belonged here at first but now feel privileged to have been part of something so positive and inspiring. Can't wait to tell everyone!'

---

strengthen a sense of peer accountability and the concept of teacher as reflective practitioner. The presentations included much showing and sharing of classroom materials, and examples of work by pupils. The projects covered the following topics, amongst others:

- raising African-Caribbean achievement, and in this connection a focus on teacher-pupil interaction, and issues of personal and collective identity and history

- working with parents and the community to ensure real partnership in education.

- Black History Month as a focus for change at school level

- setting up a whole-school system for assessing and addressing EAL needs

- race equality and accelerated learning

- working with the Somali community and induction of refugee children

- tackling racist behaviour and attitudes amongst pupils and in the local community

- involving a whole staff in analysis and action to address institutional racism

- induction programmes for newly arrived students in a secondary school.

In the final session participants considered the key stories from the workshop that they would take back to their colleagues. This was mainly through structured exchanges in threes but also through the notes they jotted. The jottings included:

> It was a fantastic opportunity to meet other schools in the borough and share good ideas and develop them together. Sharing good practice (and mistakes!) is the only way forward.

> I've learned that there are a lot of people out there who have similar views regarding the education of all children and are concerned, very much, for the children the system is failing. It's nice to have the time to discover this and realise that you are not alone and that things can change. Everyone I have spoken to has been positive and supportive and many have been able to offer help with our project, as we have offered to help with theirs where we can.

> Having the opportunity to share a wealth of ideas and suggestions has given me a real purpose to what I am doing and what my role within a school is.

In the following months there were several courses, conferences, workshops and staff meetings in individual schools, to take the programme further. In due course there was a further 24-hours residential workshop. It was again highly participatory in its structure and programming, and again some of materials are featured here. Out of this came a desire to document the whole project for colleagues in other schools. In response two days central training were provided by the LEA for staff to come to the borough's professional development centre and compile progress reports on what they had so far achieved. Participants interviewed each other in twos or threes, using the following questions as a prompt-list of points to cover:

- What, briefly, have you done?

- What were the issues you were seeking to address?

- What has been the impact on raising achievement?

- What has been the impact on the school generally?

- What have you learnt?

- What would you or will you do differently another time?

- What advice and warnings would you have for anyone embarking on a similar project in another school?

This book contains several extracts from the accounts that were written or started on those days. It draws also on two further projects in Oakwell that were inspired and influenced by Inclusive Classrooms, Inclusive Schools:

- A project entitled *Inspirations, Aspirations*. This included the piloting in Oakwell schools of *The Life of Stephen Lawrence* by Verna Allette Wilkins, and the subsequent launch of the book in its final form at Oakwell Town Hall

- A project on raising the achievement of African-Caribbean pupils. This included consultancies in several individual schools.

Further, the book reflects a number of other developments in Oakwell:

- Guidance to schools on the development and content of race equality policies, in accordance with the Race Relations Amendment Act

- Training sessions for the Oakwell inspection and advisory service

- The compilation of a handbook for schools entitled *Preventing and Addressing Racism*, and widespread consultation around its final draft

- The provision of guidance and advice following 11 September 2001.

Through its Education Equalities Working Party, mentioned above, Oakwell invited the Insted consultancy, based in London, to assist with the organisation of the Inclusive Classrooms, Inclusive Schools project and with the compilation of this eventual report.

Special funding: the case of the Ethnic Minority Achievement Grant

One purpose of this book is to share thoughts and experiences about the use of earmarked funding for race equality work, in particular the EMAG. What are the differences between EMAG and the funding regime it replaced, Section 11? What new opportunities has it opened up that previously were closed? In addition to appointing additional staff, as under Section 11, how else can such funds be used effectively? What should be the principal headings and references in budget lines and invoices, and what should the balance be between them? What are the respective responsibilities of headteachers, mainstream teachers, specialist staff and LEA officers?

The story outlined above and unfolded in this book reflects a set of beliefs and assumptions about how the EMAG can be, and ought to be, used. It is relevant to state these explicitly for they are of the book's essence. They are shown below.

Raising achievement and building equality

It is entirely possible, alas, to raise achievement but at the same time to create greater inequality. In the period 1990-2000, for example, research published by Ofsted showed that the gap widened between the national average on the one hand and the attainment of African-Caribbean and Pakistani-heritage pupils on the other. It is essential not only to raise achievement but also to promote equality.

The role of headteachers

The function of EMAG, therefore, should be to support whole-school institutional change, with a view not only to raising achievement but also to promoting equality. It follows that the leadership and management roles of headteachers are absolutely crucial. All the work described in this book benefited from the involvement and support of headteachers and other senior staff in schools.

The nature of racism and racisms

All forms of racism (all racisms, as the term often is) have two intertwining strands, to do respectively with colour and culture. The strands combine in different ways in different contexts. The racism experienced by people of African-Caribbean origin, for example, is different from the racism experienced by people of Pakistani origin, and both are different from racism directed against refugees and asylum-seekers. One major component in anti-Pakistani and anti-Bangladeshi racism is anti-Muslim racism, or Islamophobia. Measures to combat one kind of racism will not necessarily combat other kinds. In so far as EMAG is used for addressing racisms, concepts of racism must be sufficiently robust and flexible to encompass the full range. There is extensive discussion of racism in Chapter 6.

An essential message of the Stephen Lawrence Inquiry report is that all public bodies – including schools, LEAs and the DfES itself – contain features of institutional racism. The report of the Commission on the Future of Multi-Ethnic Britain (the Parekh Report) itemised the interacting components of institutional racism in public bodies. It is appropriate to use the EMAG resources for addressing institutional racism, and to identify the principal tasks in this respect which require funding.

IQism and multiple intelligences

One aspect of institutional racism in the education system is 'IQism' – the widely used and institutionalised discourse of 'ability', 'potential', 'aptitude' and 'intelligence'. There is an alternative body of discourse which speaks of 'multiple intelligences', 'preferred learning styles', 'effective learning', and 'accelerated learning'. This latter discourse appears promising from a race equality point of view, as from other points of view. But caution is required. For much of this discourse is in practice colour-blind and culture-blind. There is fuller discussion of these points in Chapter 4.

'Teachers in front of pupils'?

The vast majority of Section 11 funding had to be used for staffing in schools – people on the school or LEA payroll – and the staff were expected or required to spend most of their time on direct teaching. But with EMAG there is no such requirement. It is therefore desirable that a proportion of EMAG funds should be spent on training and professional development of existing staff rather than the appointment of additional staff, and on consultancy rather than employees. Also, the concept of targeting needs review: a proportion of EMAG funding should arguably be focused at classroom or department level rather than on individual pupils.

Professional development

The professional development of teachers, both as individuals and as teams and whole staffs, is essential. Such development is not primarily a matter of attending courses or training sessions but of engaging in action learning – the cyclical process of reflecting on practice, theorising about principles, testing out new ideas in real situations, and amending routine practice accordingly. Such development requires a certain level of risk-taking, and therefore a climate of mutual support and collaborative enquiry. There is full discussion of these points in Chapter 2.

Focus

In most schools the tendency is for EMAG funds to be spent primarily on EAL, and on the earliest stages of proficiency. But quite clearly EAL is not an issue in the under-achievement of African-Caribbean learners, or indeed of many bilingual learners. Compared with racism and Islamophobia, it may not be a major issue in Pakistani and Bangladeshi under-achievement. In any case schools should be consciously directing a proportion of EAL resources away from beginners and towards learners at later stages. In practice this means spending money on consultancy and professional development for mainstream staff rather than on individual pupils. There are examples of such projects in Chapter 3.

Evaluation

When EMAG started, the government announced that the new scheme would be independently evaluated. Tenders were invited from universities during 1999 and provisional decisions were made. Subsequently, however, the proposal was dropped. Objective assessment is nevertheless necessary, and a balance needs to be struck between evaluation for development and evaluation for accountability (inspection). Books such as this represent one possible approach to evaluation reports at LEA level, in so far as the purpose is to stimulate further development and improvement.

Concluding note: three core values

'Equality' in this book's title is a shorthand way of referring to the moral principle that all human beings are of equal value. The stories and experiences of all should be recognised and the dignity of all should be respected. Equal opportunities and access should be provided, with a view to moving towards increasing equality of outcome. But equality is not an absolute value – it is not sufficient on its own. It must be accompanied and qualified by two other values.

First, equality must be qualified by recognition of diversity. It is as unjust to treat people similarly when in relevant respects they are different as it is to treat them differently when in relevant respects they are similar. This is particularly obvious in matters relating to gender and disability – it is unjust to treat women as if in all respects their life-experiences, needs and interests are the same as those of men, and vice versa, and it is unjust not to make reasonable adjustments and accommodations to take account of the needs of people with disabilities.

In the fields of inter-ethnic, inter-cultural and inter-racial relationships, it is analogously unjust to be colour-blind or difference-blind, for not all people have the same narratives, life-experiences, perceptions and frames of reference. The government has recently adopted the semantic device of using a pair of terms – diversity and equality – in official documents. This usage was pioneered in local government and in the private sector. Pragmatic reasons for adopting it are provided by the EU Employment Directive, mandatory throughout the EU from December 2003.

The Canadian political philosopher Charles Taylor has linked the concept of diversity to that of recognition. The word 'recognition' in this book's sub-title is a deliberate echo of Taylor's arguments. He writes:

> Identity is partly shaped by recognition or its absence, often by the misrecognition of others, and so a person or group of people or society can suffer real damage, real distortion, if the people or society around them mirror back to them a confining or demeaning or contemptible picture of themselves. Nonrecognition or misrecognition can inflict harm, can be a form of oppression, imprisoning someone in a false, distorted and reduced mode of being.

A third essential concept in this context, implied by Taylor's reference to recognition, is that of social cohesion. Just as neither equality nor diversity is a sufficient moral value in itself, so also both need to be complemented and qualified by notions of cohesion and belonging. A democracy such as Britain needs not only to uphold the values of equality and diversity but also to be held together by certain shared values and – so far as is feasible – by certain shared imagery, symbols and stories.

This is not the same as claiming that Britishness is of long standing, or that British stories and symbols are static and non-negotiable. The reality is that the balance between equality, diversity and cohesion has always been a contest and that settlements have always been provisional. Britain has always contained competing perceptions, narratives and interests. There have been disagreements and negotiations related to class, gender, language, religion, region and nation. The emphasis that British identity and self-understanding are continually being negotiated and re-defined is made further in Chapter 5. Issues of national identity are bound to increase in importance in the future, with the mutually reinforcing pressures of globalisation, European integration, devolution from Westminster and Whitehall, migration, and increased social and moral pluralism. They are an essential and unavoidable aspect of citizenship education.

These notes on political philosophy may seem rather abstract, a far cry from the practical everyday life of schools, whether in Oakwell or anywhere else. In reality, however, they are what schools and classrooms are all about, all the time. They are the story of every teacher's professional life. How to hold a balance between treating children equally (and in that sense, all the same) while also recognising the unique identity, experiences and life-stories of each, and of the communities to which they belong, and at the same time striving to maintain a sense of a common stake in the well-being of the school community and the classroom community – this is the job of every teacher. It is the job that is explored, illustrated and celebrated through the pages of this book.

The next chapter looks at the job of teachers through reflections on how teachers themselves learn and develop.

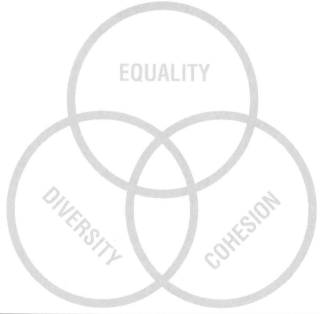

2 How Workshops Work
– the phases and process of inservice training

A real sense of purpose

'Positive and inspiring' ... 'very exciting' ... 'the conference has lifted our spirits' ... 'it has given me a real sense of purpose in what I am doing' ... 'can't wait to tell everyone' – these were some of the comments quoted in Box 3. This chapter describes, discusses and explains the kinds of inservice training activity and exercise that had evoked such enthusiasm and resolve.

Unlike most other aspects of education, training events on equality and diversity involve controversy, in the sense that there is a wide range of views amongst teachers, and an even wider and more obvious range in society at large. So there is stress. But stress arises not only because the subject matter is controversial but also because teachers may have to come to terms with their own prejudices and to change deeply-held views about themselves, about national story and history and about wider society. So inservice training in this field has to have certain distinctive characteristics. Or rather, theories and principles of professional development and continuing education are even more important in this field than in most others.

Aspects of teacher anxiety and resistance are described in Boxes 12 and 13. 'Colleagues do want to see black pupils achieve,' writes the teacher quoted in Box 12, 'but they don't know what to do. They cannot see that they are trapped within a system which reinforces underachievement and they are too scared to try and change it. A combination of curriculum workload and behaviour management issues means they don't have time for reflection. Teachers need to be encouraged and given time to challenge both their own practice and the overall system.' Similarly, the teacher quoted in Box 13 speaks of the pressures on teachers day by day, particularly the treadmill of literacy and numeracy, and the difficulties and pain of facing up to issues to do with race equality.

This chapter summarises six essential characteristics for inservice training on equality and diversity. All are of equal importance:

- Establishing and maintaining a secure base
- Providing not only security but also challenge
- Attending to case-studies and teachers' stories
- Becoming acquainted with new ideas, information and theory

- Deliberation about the implications for oneself and one's own situation
- Planning and carrying out practical projects, and reflecting on the successes achieved and the problems encountered.

At the risk of further over-simplifying, but in the hope of helping to fix the six strands in one's memory, one may name them with words all beginning with the same letter:

- Inclusion
- Incisiveness
- Inquiry
- Ideas
- Implications
- Implementation

An alternative memorising device involves using a six-letter word, as outlined in Box 14. The six elements can be helpfully grouped into three pairs – the first two are the essential tasks in a course's introductory phase, for they help to establish the collaborative climate in which effective learning takes place; the next two are the core of the course; the last two are to do with making changes in one's own professional situation. The theoretical background for the chapter as a whole is sketched in Box 4.

Establishing a secure base

Security at the start of a course is provided by a certain type of keynote lecture; by discussion exercises and tasks in small groups that are non-threatening and confidence-building; and by appealing to a range of learning styles and preferences amongst participants.

Keynote lectures

It is customary to start a course with a keynote lecture by a specialist. There is always a danger, however, that the message received by the audience (as distinct from the message intended by the lecturer) is that they are empty vessels waiting to be filled. Since in fact all members of an audience have a range of preoccupations, concerns and relevant experiences (they do not come as empty vessels), a keynote lecture can speak past them rather than to them. In consequence, people feel unrecognised and unrespected and are disinclined to attend to the lecture, let alone to engage with it. A further disadvantage of keynote lectures is that they tacitly endorse chalk-and-talk-type teaching in school classrooms.

However, plenary lectures are not intrinsically excluding. Nor is whole-class teaching. Lectures help provide security and a sense of being included if:

*   the lecturer makes it clear that he or she respects the practical knowledge and lived, professional experience of those listening

*   the lecturer shows respect for the audience by providing a clear pattern, structure and sequence for the talk

*   authors cited reflect a wide range of background

*   illustrative anecdotes and cultural references reflect a wide spectrum of experiences and assumptions

*   controversy, doubt and difficulty are acknowledged

*   jokes and humour are always inclusive

*   an overview is provided of issues to be addressed later in the course.

Box 4

Theories of professional development

The approach to inservice training and professional development outlined in this chapter is derived, directly or indirectly, from five main bodies of theory and practice.

'The Reflective Practitioner'

Donald Schon argues that teachers, in common with professionals in many other fields, learn from reflecting on their own practice and from engaging in action-research in order to change it.

Learning Styles theory

David Kolb and his co-workers have similarly focused on the relationship between theory and practice, and have described learning as a continual circle involving (a) practice (b) reflection (c) theory and (d) action. They maintain that each individual is stronger in some than in others, and that four distinct learning styles can be identified.

Group Dynamics theory

Kurt Lewin developed T-groups in the 1940s and 1950s, originally with a therapeutic purpose. The groups were developed in England by the Tavistock Institute and the Grubb Institute, both based in London, for training senior professionals. In watered-down versions the techniques have been widely used in 'human awareness training' (HAT) in the public and private sectors and they have affected the methodology used in training courses for teachers.

Conscientisation theory

Paulo Freire and his followers, initially based in South American countries, developed a strong body of theory and related methodology which is often referred to as 'conscientisation' or 'pedagogy of the oppressed'. This too stressed the relationship between theory and practice, but had an explicitly radical political position, and was (and is) far more radical than the other theoretical frameworks outlined here.

Racism Awareness Training

This grew out of HAT (see above) and is associated with the name of Judith Katz in the United States. It was developed by the National Union of Teachers in England in the early 1980s and exerted considerable influence. Around 1987, however, it came under sustained attack from more radical viewpoints, on the grounds that it was concerned only with individual change not structural or institutional change. It was strongly recommended in the Stephen Lawrence Inquiry report, but is nevertheless rare.

For bibliographical details, see page 91.

Discussion tasks in small groups

Security is provided not only by the content and tone of lectures but also by opportunities for reflective discussion in pairs or small groups. The maximum size for group discussion aiming to provide security is probably six – though certainly groups can be larger if they have a skilled facilitator who ensures that all members of the group participate fully and that everyone has a fair hearing.

In the early part of a course, discussion needs to be structured rather than open – there needs to be a task to engage in and complete, not just a vague invitation to talk. Two useful pieces of material for structured discussion are included here as Box 5 'Where We Are Coming From' and Box 6 'Events and Experiences over the Years'. The exercises are alternatives to each other, for few courses could find time for both. In each, course members are asked first to jot notes. These are for their own eyes only and are to help them collect their thoughts. For it is easier to select, share and express one's thoughts if one has first gathered them together. Also it is easier to attend to other people's thoughts and selections, and to consider them non-judgementally, if one has previously sorted one's own. After this, course members talk about themselves in pairs or small groups. The following results are likely to be achieved:

- Participants are reassured that their own experience is valid and relevant, and so have a sense that they are respected and trusted

- They reflect on their own personal and professional experience by comparing and contrasting it with that of others, and are therefore more open to modifying and developing their views and understandings

- They are reminded of aspects of diversity within the teaching profession, for example to do with cultural, class and geographical background

- They are tacitly reminded that it is not only teachers who need to feel secure and that their background is recognised and respected but also pupils.

In the one introductory exercise (Box 5) the focus is on four dimensions of identity and belonging – geography, space and region; ethnicity, culture and race; social class; and specific professional and personal

---

Box 5

Where we're coming from

Please jot notes under the four headings below. The notes are private *aide-memoires*, to help us collect our thoughts before talking about aspects of personal identity and belonging.

In terms of geography, region, place ...

Where born and grew up ... parents and grandparents ... what you like and don't like, if anything, about the places where you have lived ...

In terms of ethnicity, culture, colour and race ...

Some words to describe yourself ... what you like and don't like, if anything, about your culture and race

In terms of social class

How you would describe yourself ... whether you have changed, or are changing ... what you like and don't like, if anything, about your class position ...

In terms of experience

Things you've done, things that have happened to you, relevant to the subject-matter of today's discussions

---

experiences. Talk amongst colleagues on these four dimensions is invariably illuminating. Amongst other things, it usually dispels 'majority/minority discourse' – the twin notions that all white people are alike since they are white and that all Asian and black people are alike since they are not. The point is obvious but nevertheless worth rehearsing and repeating – there are many significant ways in which human beings differ, and skin colour and cultural heritage are only two amongst many. Others include geography, gender, age, religion, class, political ideology, personal ethics and lifestyle, profession and occupation. Recognising diversity within the teaching profession is an important step towards recognising diversity amongst pupils.

In the alternative introductory exercise (Box 6), the focus is more obviously sequential. Participants are asked to cast their minds back over their lives and to recall events and experiences which, from the vantage point of today's inservice event, appear significant. The

Box 6

Events and experiences over the years

Please jot notes under the four headings below. The notes are private *aide-memoires*, to help us collect our thoughts before talking about aspects of our education and background. In each instance mention things that you did or that happened to you which seem significant in the light of today's discussions.

Before the age of 12

Teenage years and young adulthood

Since the age of about 25

During the last ten days

suggested categories, to assist preliminary sorting, are memories of childhood; memories of teenage years and early adulthood; memories over the years; and things that have happened in the immediate past. When teachers recall experiences they had when they were young themselves they are reminded of positive experiences they would like their current pupils to have, and negative experiences they would like their pupils to be spared.

Either introductory exercise is valuable for helping to build a collaborative climate of mutual respect and trust amongst the participants, such that they are more ready to engage in learning. For learning, in the case of professional adults as well as pupils and students, involves readiness to be confronted and challenged, and therefore to take risks.

The big picture

A gentle way of introducing a measure of challenge after one of the exercises in Boxes 5 and 6 is to provide a set of quotations, for example those in Box 7. These are from letters and submissions made to the Commission on the Future of Multi-Ethnic Britain, and quoted in its report. Between them, they sketch out the issues explored in greater detail in later chapters of this book – issues of personal and national identity; intercultural relations and contacts; concepts of equality, difference and cohesion; and action against racism in its various forms.

The quotations can be presented all together on a single sheet, as in Box 7. Alternatively each can be presented on its own card or slip of paper, so that participants literally handle and sort the quotations and exercise control and choice. Either way there needs to be a simple task to focus thinking and discussion. For example, 'choose the quotation you think provides the best introduction to the subject-matter of this course'. Or, 'select the three quotations which you find most interesting'. It is valuable if participants first engage in the task alone before they work with others.

The effect is to give a sense of 'the big picture'. This helps to reinforce security, since the subject-matter, though vast, is made to seem manageable. At the same time the exercise is challenging, since controversial and sensitive ideas and topics are on the table and choices have to be made.

More elaborate ways of using quotations include the complementary use of visual material – postcards of various kinds, for example, or photographs or cartoons. Participants choose not only quotations which catch their attention but also images. The juxtaposition of words and images adds richness and texture, and arguably involves people more fully than do words alone. Other ways include various kinds of card game – the quotations are 'dealt' out, and participants exchange, select and 'discard' in order each to get the best possible 'hand'.

Learning styles

It is important to be sensitive to different learning styles. Some participants will enjoy and learn from talks and lectures, whereas others need to talk and discuss with each other in small groups. Some people are helped by visual material and by metaphors, symbols and stories, whereas others are more comfortable with unambiguous prose. People feel respected and trusted if their preferred ways of learning are recognised, but feel challenged and intrigued, as distinct from merely irritated or alienated, if other styles are affirmed as well. (A participant at one of the Oakwell residential workshops remarked on her evaluation form that she hadn't enjoyed the touchy-feely exercises, as she called them, on the first evening. At the same time she acknowledged that other participants had clearly appreciated them. She noted that her own views were perhaps conditioned by her experience as a secondary

Box 7

Issues in multi-ethnic Britain

The future of Britain

The future of Britain lies in the hands of descendants of slave owners and slaves, of indentured labourers, of feudal landlords and serfs, of industrialists and factory workers, of lairds and crofters, of refugees and asylum-seekers.

'Not yet, not yet'

I still think of that scene at the end of *A Passage to India*, where two characters discuss relations between English and Indian people and say 'Not yet, not yet' with regard to full understanding. I think one could say the same about relationships between all the communities in Great Britain and do not think we can hope for anything more than a distant mutual toleration.

Our problem

The Rule Britannia mindset, given full-blown expression at the *Last Night of the Proms* and until recently at the start of programming each day on BBC Radio 4, is a major part of the problem of Britain. In the same way that it continues to fight the Second World War ... Britain seems incapable of shaking off its imperialist identity. The Brits do appear to believe that 'Britons never, never, never shall be slaves'. But it is impossible to colonise three-fifths of the world without enslaving oneself. Our problem has been that Britain has never understood itself and has steadfastly refused to see and understand itself through the prism of our experience of it, here and in its coloniser mode.

Underclass

Rather than concentrate on minorities based on ethnicity or religion, should we not urge Government increasingly to counter the emergence of an underclass, whose deepening exclusion – known to every youth magistrate – is a matter of shame to the whole nation? Of course this underclass has black, Asian (mainly Muslim) and white minorities within it – but it is the pains, injustices and problems of the underclass as a whole which require fundamental action. It is here that the questions of racism, equalities, etc, take on their sharpest edge.

No budget

One hospital was rather surprised when I sent them an invoice following a six-hour interpreting session on a serious case involving complicated diagnosis and treatment. They said they never paid for interpreting as they have no budget for such things. When I asked how they managed with translations, 'We use relatives' was the reply. 'And if there are no relatives?' I enquired. 'We use cleaners,' said the head nurse.

Not going to accept that

We came here because they brought us over here to do the jobs that they didn't want to do and now that we've made something of our life they're cursing us for it. They want us to go back because they've finished with us. We're not going to accept that, we're going to make ourselves better. We're going to strive to make our community better than what it is already. And we're always going to do that.

Most hated

There was a newspaper article about racism. It asked a hundred white people about it – and most hated was Asians, Muslims. That makes me realise I'm walking around now and people are looking at me in a different way.

'Tolerant' society

There is a tendency in western democracies to believe that secular society provides the best public space for equality and tolerance ... [but] secular society tends to push religion ... to the margins of public space and into the private sphere. Islamophobia and antisemitism merge with a more widespread rejection of religion which runs through a significant part of 'tolerant society', including the educated middle class and the progressive media.

Taking responsibility

Racism is often portrayed as though it is something like a disease which can be cured. Racist beliefs are reinforced in so many ways in white people, from the cradle onwards. It's not a question of curing me, but of me acknowledging my racism and taking responsibility for operating in an anti-racist way personally and encouraging organisations and institutions in which I have an influence to do the same.

Source: Letters, statements and evidence quoted in *The Future of Multi-Ethnic Britain*, Profile Books, 2000.

Box 8

Sorry – frequently offered excuses

One may hear comments about race equality issues in education from colleagues like these. Mark three of them, and consider how you would respond and the discussions that might develop.

Time

'There isn't time for it. We must concentrate on more basic things, particularly if we want to be as high as possible in the league tables.'

Knowledge

I'm not an expert on this, and don't even know where I can find out what I need to know. I'd rather play from my strenghs, not reveal my weaknesses.'

Disagreement

'It will open up a can of worms, and we'll all end up arguing and disagreeing with each other, and generally becoming demoralised.'

No problem here

'It isn't relevant at our school. We have very few pupils from minority backgrounds and they all seem perfectly happy.'

No textbooks

'There aren't any decent textbooks or other materials, so we're going to have to write our own, and there isn't time.'

Upsetting for pupils

'It will make the pupils uncomfortable. They're much happier if we treat them all the same.'

PC gone mad

'It's political correctness gone mad. We should just keep to the school development plan.'

Similarities

'We should teach about similarities, and what all people have in common, not about differences.'

Doing it already

'We do slavery and black history month, there's really no need for anything more.'

---

teacher, and stressed that the benefits of being in a discussion group with primary colleagues had far outweighed the discomfort of having to be less cerebral and verbal than was her natural inclination.) There is further discussion of learning style theory in Chapter 4.

From security to challenge

Security without challenge, controversy and disagreement is mere complacency. It is important, once a basic climate of trust has been established, to provide tasks that require the exchange of different points of view. The overall purpose is not necessarily to move towards consensus, if this means that everyone should come to hold the same opinion. Rather, the purpose is to build a climate of collaboration in which participants seek to clarify their own thinking by comparing and contrasting their ideas and perceptions with those of others.

In the following paragraphs there are notes on four possible activities: to do respectively with frequently offered excuses ('FOES'); critical comments about their education from pupils; stories about real or imaginary situations requiring both an immediate and a longer-term response; and role-playing a staff meeting or governors meeting.

FOES – Frequently Offered Excuses

Box 8 contains comments familiar in almost any staffroom or meeting of governors. The thoughts and feelings here may also be in the minds of participants at a training event, though unvoiced. It is important that teachers should feel confident in responding to them. One way of starting to use the material at a training event is to ask each individual to select the three comments they find most difficult to cope with. Discussion and clarification then aim to establish general principles.

More elaborately, the comments can be used in simple role-plays of professional conversations. One useful format in this connection is to work in threes. In each three, one person takes the part of someone who sympathises with the comment; a second takes the part of someone who disagrees, but who tries to engage in constructive conversation as distinct from mere argument; and the third acts as an observer and makes notes. The role-played conversation runs for 5-10 minutes at most, followed by reflection on what emerged.

Several of the FOES in Box 8 express or imply low expectations of pupils. It is therefore relevant to link them to the discussion of teacher expectations in Chapter 4. Also, they have much in common with the concerns and experiences of the teachers cited in Boxes 12 and 13 and resonate with the challenging voices of pupils heard in Box 9.

How it was at school

Box 9 contains comments by young people looking back on their schooldays. All are critical and challenge the professional self-esteem of teachers. One way of using such quotations at a training session is to provide them on separate slips of paper. They are dealt out at random and participants read them out to each other. The group then agrees on the three or four they would like to consider in detail. Discussion will raise many questions, including the following:

- With which of these comments do we ourselves empathise most strongly?

- Which do we find most difficult to identify with?

- What specific incidents may have triggered off these feelings and views?

- How should teachers respond to such incidents so that feelings of bitterness, anger and exclusion are not aggravated and strengthened?

- Do the pupils we ourselves teach have such feelings, or may they have such feelings in the future?

- How do we know?

- What are we going to do about it?

The comments in Box 9 are all in their various ways about the expectations that the young people quoted felt that their schools had of them. There is extensive discussion of teacher expectations in Chapter 4.

To be continued

Stories such as those in Box 10 have the following uses:

- If used near the start of a course or meeting, they give participants reassurance that the programme ahead is going to be down-to-earth, and that it is likely to help them solve or manage the practical problems of their everyday work.

- They encode challenging ideas and arguments, and therefore encourage debate and disagreement.

- They provide a useful reminder that even the best prepared plans can go wrong, and that unforeseen problems often arise. Successful change in education, as in other areas of work, requires amongst other things that there should be frank acknowledgement of uncertainties and failures, and realistic anticipation of resistance and difficulty.

- They provide pegs on which to hang theoretical discussion, and therefore they make communication easier. They can be referred to directly during a course, for example in talks and lectures, and also in conversation.

- By omitting much basic detail, they invite discussion of underlying issues and causes, and of long-term plans for substantial institutional change.

- They invite attention to the ways in which they themselves are constructed and narrated. Has the person telling the story misunderstood his or her situation? How might a different person narrate the same episode?

Box 9

How it was at school

'The overriding feeling was a sense of injustice at the fact that everything about the content and structure of the curriculum seemed to be saying that black people are worthless at best, never had amounted to anything and never would without the white man.'

'The way certain teachers reacted to me or dealt with me was coming from a fixed attitude they had, and I would say it was more of not looking at that person (me) in particular. It was more coming from a textbook, like only on the surface, only on the surface, like a robot, not looking at you as a person.'

'We had Development Studies in history. I was taught that people in Ghana wore grass skirts and lived in mud huts until the white man came with intermediate technology.'

"When I was in the juniors they used to call me names in the playground all the time, like 'nigger'. They used to upset me and sometimes I would get so mad I would fight and then I would get in trouble. I was always the one who got in trouble. They didn't do nothing to the ones that was doing it. They sent me to the head. I was crying and he told me that I mustn't fight, he said it didn't mean anything, everybody gets called names and I must rise above it. But they still kept on doing it.'

'There was BNP marches and language like 'wog' and 'nigger' being used and I got the feeling that the world doesn't want me and I don't want it either. It can get stuffed.'

'You were forced into it. If you were black you were a target for racists. You are identified as a target and it comes to you. I don't know a single black person who hasn't been attacked at least verbally, and most physically. If you are a white person you can choose to be a racist at weekends and not show it during the week. It is optional whether you are involved in this stuff. It is optional whether you take it seriously.'

'The teachers were mostly white. You can't look at a white person and tell if they are a racist, so if they haven't told you their views you can't go to a white person and complain about white racism.'

'I was given extra English support and the teacher was great. The trouble was that it wasn't linked to any of the topics I was covering in class ... There was no attempt to integrate it. In history, geography and English no attempt was made to integrate me.'

'We had a black head who was tough but fair. You felt he really cared what happened to you. I went through a bad time. I was separated from my family, I was picked on and there was a lot of bullying. I wasn't able to express how I felt so I took matters into my own hands. I was suspended on a number of occasions ... You need a range of role models in a school that show the complexity and diversity of people's lives. My head teacher was a positive role model for me.'

'There was a lot of name-calling and fights. There were no black teachers at the school and no acknowledgement of black experience. No black history was taught, for example.'

'There was setting in maths and it was bad. It sent the wrong messages – of lower expectations for certain groups. You don't get stretched. You need to be challenged in school. You need excitement and external influences.'

'There was nothing I could relate to at school about my ethnic identity and me ... This came through English and history lessons. I felt they projected a negative image of my country of origin and this affected my status in the school.'

Sources: various former Oakwell students, and voices cited in *The Future of Multi-Ethnic Britain*

They encourage a spirit of collaborative enquiry, such that participants feel keen to find out more and think more deeply about underlying issues. In these ways they provide a useful introduction to the next stage of the course.

The following notes comment on the four stories in Box 10. They show the kinds of issue that are likely to arise and to be discussed, and the general principles that are likely to emerge.

With regard to the first story, it is important that teachers should recognise and accept that black British people, and indeed black people throughout the world, have feelings of anger and bitterness about the history of slavery. In this story the teacher seems to have been in denial over how the pupil feels, and is therefore unable to respond to the pupil with appropriate professionalism, as distinct from personal pique and defensiveness. The teacher could quite easily have reflected back the pupil's feelings by saying something like 'you feel strongly, don't you? and this would probably have opened up and supported a valuable, educative conversation.

The pupil needs to be able to talk about the episode to a sympathetic adult, so that legitimate disappointment about the teacher's indifference and lack of understanding does not fester into deeper feelings of alienation and disaffection. The adult the pupil speaks to may then be able to act as an advocate with the headteacher or another senior member of staff, and this may valuably lead to staff training about the perceptions, stories and experiences of black British communities and individuals, and to significant changes in the curriculum and school ethos. It is essential, in teaching about slavery, to emphasise the great African civilisations that were established long before the slave trade started, and to stress stories of survival, resistance, determination and hope.

The important point to draw from the second story is that racist name-calling is different from, and much more serious than, the other kinds of insult that children and young people trade with each other. The first thing the teacher needs to do here, therefore, is to confirm to the child that terms such as 'Paki', even when used in jest or in ignorance, have their history and implications and are totally unacceptable. Also the teacher needs to affirm that the child was right to mention the episode – reporting it was not a matter of 'telling tales'.

Box 10

To be continued

What next?

I'm in Year 6. This week I wrote a poem about slavery. 'It's well expressed,' said the teacher, who's white, ' but terribly extreme. You don't really feel like that, do you?' – 'Of course I do,' I said. 'We all do. I'm angry about what you people did to us, and you're still doing it.' – 'It wasn't me that did it,' snapped the teacher, raising her voice, 'and any way I don't like the way you're talking to me about this.' And that was that. What next?

Not nice

I'm a newly qualified teacher. This week, my first week of teaching, a child came into the classroom after break mentioning matter-of-factly that another child had called her a stupid Paki. 'That's not nice,' she said, 'is it?' – 'No,' I said. 'So how can I get my own back?' she asked.

Multicultural stuff

I'm the head of an infants school. I showed a few prospective parents round the school yesterday evening. After we had seen the classrooms and the hall, one of them asked if she could have a word with me in private. 'Look,' she said, 'I must be honest with you, I've heard some worrying things about this place. They say you do too much of that multicultural stuff. I'd like Sarah to come here, but I've got to reassure my husband. You do have a proper Nativity play, don't you, and you teach correct English, and you don't teach Pakistani?'

'They don't really understand'

I'm the parent of children aged 4 and 6. They were desperately distressed by the TV footage on 11 September. I spoke to their class teachers. Both said much the same: 'Yes, a lot of the children seem quite upset. But they'll soon get over it. They don't really understand, you know. Don't worry.'

The child's desire to retaliate needs to be recognised, not swept under the carpet. There are plenty of wounding epithets that could be used in reply – though the teacher will probably not wish to provide a list of them! But certainly the teacher needs to support the child's desire to be assertive and to sort out problems in the playground for herself. One sort of assertive reply, for example, would be along the lines of 'I'm really proud to be British Pakistani, and you would be too if you were me.'

The staff of the school (including administrative and support staff) need to discuss the episode and other similar episodes. The very process of discussing a story such as this reflectively, and considering various angles on it, is likely to be illuminating. Staff training sessions should therefore feature discussion of such stories. Out of such discussion will come consensus on the unacceptability of racist terms and how to explain this to all children. There is fuller discussion of dealing with racist incidents in Chapter 6.

In the third story, the headteacher must communicate to the parent that she (the parent) has been heard and understood. Many white people do feel a sense of dispossession and dislocation in modern society, and mistakenly attribute this to 'immigrants'. The headteacher needs to show empathy with the feelings, though not agreement or endorsement. The head needs also to assert without apology that the school is

---

Box 11

Views and voices at a meeting

Role-cards for a governors meeting. The agenda item is whether to adopt into the staff handbook some material on racist incidents issued by the LEA.

Hostile

You consider that there is much too much political correctness around, and that this paper is a prime example. Children insult each other all the time, they always have and they always will, and calling someone Paki is no worse than calling someone Fatty. The school should be concentrating on the 3Rs, not wasting time with so-called antiracism. You are quick to take offence, particularly if anyone accuses you, or appears to accuse you, of being racist.

Avoidance

Secretly you are against this paper, for you think it will do more harm than good. The paper smacks of political correctness, and you do not think that so-called racist insults are any worse than other kinds of insult. And any way children don't understand what they're saying, they don't mean to be vicious, they just repeat what they have heard their parents say ... However, you don't say any of this explicitly. You simply try to divert attention to other matters. You will be successful in this role-play if you can get the group to discuss, preferably in great detail, various red herrings.

Constructively critical

You are strongly in favour of incorporating this material into the staff handbook. But you want it to be improved, if at all possible. At the very least you want every item to be fully discussed and you want to be confident that each item means the same thing to different people. You are inclined to be impatient with people who don't agree with you and you may well, in this discussion, accuse them of being racist.

Supportive

You are strongly in favour of incorporating this material into the staff handbook. However, it is important in your view that there should be as much consensus as possible. So you try to be supportive not only of the material itself but also of the other members of the group, even if you do not agree with them. Try to get them to change their minds, if you think they are wrong, but do this by showing that you understand where they're coming from. Try not to be confrontational, and to be supportive towards anyone who is distressed or uncomfortable.

multicultural and is proud to be so. The parent's mistaken assumptions (for example that there is a language called Pakistani) should be gently corrected. But the main thing is to invite her to come and see for herself how valuable multicultural education is for all children, and to see how fortunate she and her family are to be involved with a multicultural school.

With regard to the fourth story, young children in September 2001 did understand that something terrible had happened. It was difficult or impossible to prevent them seeing the coverage on television, but in any case they were aware that their parents and carers were troubled. The teacher here is in denial, possibly because she herself cannot understand – though who could? – what had happened.

The parent needs to speak to the headteacher, and there needs to be a staff discussion. Various organisations, particularly in the United States, provided helpful guidance to teachers, carers and parents on talking to children and young people about 11 September, much of it available on the Internet. A copy of the guidance circulated to schools in Oakwell, based closely on a document developed at Purdue University, is shown in Box 40.

Role-play

The stories in Box 10 lend themselves to simple role-played professional conversations, as outlined above in the discussion of FOES. A more elaborate form of role-play is to imagine a staff meeting or governors' meeting and to provide role-cards for some of the participants. The four cards in Box 11 were prepared for an imaginary governors' meeting at which there was discussion about incorporating into the staff handbook some guidelines on dealing with racist incidents. At the end of such role-play it is essential that there should be substantial discussion of how people felt, particularly those who took on roles they would not play in real life, and of the principles that have been learnt for dealing with real life.

Considering case-studies and teachers' stories

In all inservice training it is extremely valuable for teachers to describe work they themselves have done. Typically, they explain their thoughts and concerns before a project started; how they set about planning; what resources and materials they used; how the pupils responded; and what the results were. There are boxes throughout this book that contain stories and accounts from practising teachers. The two in this chapter are entitled 'I do believe individuals can make a difference' and 'I'm meant to be writing up a report'. They have in common that they stress that change in schools in relation to issues of equality and diversity is always complex, frequently difficult and sometimes all but impossible. They describe poignantly the constraints and obstacles that can be encountered, and the resistance amongst colleagues than can arise even from well planned and organised training sessions. Both accounts are painfully honest. Small details in them have been altered to prevent the schools being identified.

How the two texts came into being is of interest. The first started with an oral report to a small group of colleagues at a training event and the teacher then dictated the story to someone acting as scribe. There was discussion between the teacher and the scribe to clarify points of detail and find the best words. The second text is edited down from the transcript of a teacher talking to three others at a training event.

More obviously than any of the other stories in this book, the story in Box 13 is a snapshot in time – it is blatantly and tantalisingly unfinished. It is printed in this form, rather than with a neat and tidy resolution, for the sake of honesty. When the words were first spoken they did indeed peter out, as Box 13 indicates. Also, it is honest to acknowledge in a book such as this that people do sometimes run up against a brick wall, and feel that there is no way through or ahead.

The story starts impressively and the description of a half-day training event shows considerable imagination and commitment. But it ends up lamely in uncertainty and a sense of defeat. The reader is left to wonder what happened next – the school did in fact find a way through, due to the determination and leadership of the headteacher and the professionalism and commitment of the staff and the external consultant.

Box 12

I do believe individuals can make a difference

A real challenge

Working within a strong multi-ethnic school that was genuinely proud of its wide range of language groups and its diverse population, I expected to be able to build on the good practice in order to focus in particular on issues of African-Caribbean achievement. But what I found was that the school was only happy for me to work up a project, and implement it, if it didn't challenge the school's own systems.

I think schools want to be seen to be doing race equality work and in their own minds the 'saris, samosas and steel bands approach' is radical enough. Something that has got African-Caribbean achievement in the title, and focuses on just a single ethnic group, is a real challenge for people who believe that equal opportunity can be achieved by treating all people the same, rather than responding to individual needs. And as soon as it becomes clear that a project will explore racism and expose the weaknesses of a school's systems, they back off. They dare not face up to the racism that schools perpetuate.

Our own labelling

There was a perception within one school where I worked that African-Caribbean pupils were a problem as far as behaviour management was concerned. There was still a strong feeling amongst staff that black pupils were operating in gangs and were more lippy than white pupils. So when I began to try to tackle issues around perceptions of black pupils' behaviour people got very defensive. What I was trying to say was that although black pupils in the school do not cause more problems than anyone else the mythology surrounding them labels them as trouble. It's our own labelling that needs to be addressed in the first instance, not the behaviour of the pupils.

It wasn't just the senior management who got agitated when I began to focus on the black pupils. Colleagues at a peer level tended to take the issues personally and feel that the guilt of the world's racism rested on their shoulders. They felt that they were accused of being racist, when the real issue is how to move forward towards a fairer society.

They said they didn't want to be involved in something that appeared to 'reward bad behaviour.' I tried to unpick the kind of thinking behind that statement and I think it reveals a genuine insecurity about the race equality agenda. Colleagues who say such things have internalised the view that black pupils are trouble and feel that it is such an obvious fact that to begin talking to those very same pupils about the racism they face in wider society would simply be to give them a platform for their grievances, and would undermine the position of teachers.

Go for it

A school needs to 'go for it', I believe, and name the problem – staff need to understand why they find the behaviour of black pupils particularly challenging. I have seen interactions that begin with the usual static of teenagers escalate into dangerous challenges to the teacher's authority simply because the child is black. I have watched teachers wind kids up so that they do act inappropriately.

So teachers are resentful that pupils whom they perceive as 'bad' are getting 'good' things. They feel they have done all they can to accommodate the 'learning styles' of such pupils. They have 'bent over backwards' for black pupils and feel now that only punitive measures will work. Their mistake is to think that the pupils themselves are the problem, and not the system.

So we spend our time in tokenistic gestures which don't improve attainment and don't really tackle the alienation of black pupils within the school system. And I suppose I have come to believe that that is a definition of institutional racism which perhaps goes a bit deeper than the formalised language of the Lawrence Inquiry report.

Box 12 continued

You can dare to listen

But before we sink into hopeless despair and beat our breasts saying 'woe is me, what can be done about the race equality agenda?' let me stress that I do believe individuals can make a difference. Perhaps it is aiming too high to bash the system into submission and deconstruct what it has taken decades, even centuries, to establish. But you can bring in black writers and poets, black learning mentors and black members of staff. You can dare to listen to your black kids. You can provide space for them to find empowerment as they face the racism outside of school.

And it has an effect. Sitting in an assembly watching pupils celebrate Diwali, listening to pupils' lively discussion of their visit to the play about the Lawrence Inquiry, or reading work with a class by black British poets about their day-to-day life experiences, all have a drip-feed effect. Senior management are happy, because they can say 'Look, we're celebrating our multicultural diversity.' And those of us looking for something more, that elusive vision of racial justice, can see minds challenged and hopefully a future generation better equipped in terms of both knowledge and experience to take the struggle on.

What I mean by this is that teachers do want to see black pupils achieve but they don't know what to do. They cannot see that they are trapped within a system which reinforces underachievement and they are too scared to try and change it. A combination of curriculum workload and behaviour management issues means they don't have time for reflection. Teachers need to be encouraged and given time to challenge both their own practice and the overall system.

National issue

It's all to do with this 'naming the problem'. Society as a whole has to take responsibility for racism. Individual teachers need to be reassured that the difficulties they face in their classrooms and in their schools are part of a much broader picture that needs to be challenged at a fundamental level. Underachievement of black pupils is a national issue and it should be safe to discuss it, dissect it and strategise how to deal with it. Teachers are often undervalued for this kind of approach, when actually they should be praised for their work.

Within any school community there is a diversity of thought about how a problem should be tackled and indeed what caused it in the first place. It's rare to find an out and out racist who will say 'Well it's because they're black, and that's all there is to it.' The usual range is 'I'd like to do more about race equality, but I haven't got the time.' 'All children are important, why just concentrate on a few?' and 'The black pupils in the school are already running the place, they don't need any more assertiveness training.' It is much easier to say that 'Trevor is just a bad boy' than it is to unpick what makes him a bad character in the eyes of white society. And when you try to do that, that's when you open the can of worms.

Well, is bottom-up antiracism, starting with the individual teacher, really possible? I would say that yes it is, but it cannot be done in isolation. If you are a single individual teacher you need to seek out allies, either within the school or wider world, so that you can challenge the system together.

Box 13

I'm meant to be writing up a report

A working definition

After the Town Hall conference I decided to tackle the problem of African-Caribbean under-achievement. The first question was, were the black pupils under-achieving and how could we find out? The statistics we had were incomplete and unreliable.

It was agreed that we would start by setting aside a half-day training session. In preparation for this I asked all staff to give me a list of pupils in their class who were in their view under-achieving. I didn't attempt to define under-achievement, and one result of this was there was a lot of confusion with children on the SEN register. And I didn't mention that I was interested in race. I just asked for the lists of names and decided to accept what everybody put.

At the training session the first thing we did was try to agree a working definition. It was incredibly difficult, but we got something together in the end. This is what we said:

> A pupil at this school may be identified as under-achieving if, in the teacher's professional judgement, he or she has demonstrated an ability to achieve, but is failing to reach expectations and therefore to maximise potential. Identification of underachievement may be based on assessment of classroom work or observation of classroom behaviour. Indicators of under-achievement include verbal confidence but low standards of written work, significant variations of achievement in different subjects, most importantly in English and Maths, and failure to show expected progress.

That was as tight as we could make it. And then we went on to look at causes, and then at procedures, and then at strategies. All this was impressive, particularly the list of strategies.

Problem

It was then and only then that I raised the question of race. I pointed out that approximately half the children identified by the staff as under-achieving by their own definition, and in need of intervention strategies of the kind they themselves had proposed, were African-Caribbean – whereas the actual proportion of African-Caribbean kids in the school as a whole was only 10 per cent. Colleagues were shocked and had to agree that the school had a problem.

From the strategies the staff had agreed on, I proposed a mentoring scheme. I arranged for a learning support assistant, himself of African-Caribbean background, to work with the pupils on a one-to-one basis, and I offered to cover classes so that colleagues could have personal consultations with him. There was massive resistance and inertia. Why pick on black kids, people asked. Very few took up my offer to cover their classes. The general line was that they have too many other things to do – literacy and numeracy and so forth. I was very disappointed.

All racist

Well, what we did then was arrange for a consultant to come in and talk to staff. I couldn't be there, unfortunately, the day he came, and I don't know exactly what happened. But what people told me was he'd told them that whether they knew it or not they were all racist. I asked him for his own perception of the meeting and he agreed there had been enormous resistance. One member of staff had said to him 'I don't know where you've got the idea from that African-Caribbean pupils at this school are under-achieving, because they're not.'

He couldn't understand it, and I can't understand it, and I don't know what to do. Colleagues deny that there's a problem and they're furious that they think they have been accused of racism. They're refusing to have anything more to do with the consultant.

One factor is that there are four kids at the school with mega behaviour difficulties, and it so happens they're all black. They have a very high profile, and it's as if because of these four, and because staff don't know how to handle them, they're not prepared to consider under-achievement amongst any of the black kids at the school.

Just at the moment

What worries me just at the moment is that I'm meant to be writing up a report about the project, and I've got nothing to say! We've got nowhere. I simply don't know what to do.

Source: shortened and edited transcript of a teacher talking in a small group.

Becoming acquainted with new information and theory

Teachers on a course need a certain amount of new information. But information alone is not enough. They need also, as the stories in Boxes 12 and 13 make clear, to develop and strengthen attitudes of respect and sympathy for the full range of their pupils, and to confront prejudices and resistance within themselves and each other. They need therefore to become acquainted with theories and perspectives developed by significant thinkers over the years – there is nothing so practical, it has been said, as a sound theory. Key concepts include:

- Culture, and inter-cultural relationships and communications.

- The power of teacher expectations and related issues to do with concepts of ability and intelligence, with teacher-pupil interaction and relationships, and with learning style theory and accelerated learning.

- The nature of racism – its causes and effects, the various forms it takes, and practical ways to prevent and address it in schools.

- National history and identity, and ways of giving all pupils a sense of belonging and having a stake in the future.

- Language – including in particular the differences between everyday English and curriculum English, and ways of supporting pupils for whom English is an additional language.

- Globalisation and its effects.

- The role of the mass media.

- Gender – the ways in which the experiences, interests and perceptions of women are different, from those of men in every community and in mainstream society.

Some of these topics, though not all, are dealt with later in this book. See Chapter 3 for references to language policy; Chapter 4 for discussions of teacher expectations and related issues; Chapter 5 for discussions of identity, community and nation; and Chapter 6 on tackling racism in its various forms. In all these chapters there are activities and exercises designed to extend teachers' knowledge and understanding of important theoretical concepts.

Deliberation about implications for oneself

Information and academic theory are important. But they must be discussed, and must affect action. They must therefore be translated into statements of principles which will influence practice.

This book contains many examples of such statements. They include the statement in Box 22 about children new to English; the observations in Box 28 about intelligence; the statement about British history quoted in Box 33; and the model school policy on race equality in Box 49. Further, there are summarising statements about the Ethnic Minority Achievement Grant in Chapter 1; the benefits of accelerated learning and the effects of teacher expectations in Chapter 4; Britain pictured as a 'community of communities' in Chapter 5; and the nature of racism and dealing with racist incidents in Chapter 6. The present chapter is a summarising statement, illustrated with a range of examples, of principles underlying the organisation of inservice training.

Planning and carrying out projects

Ideally an inservice course should include opportunities for teachers to engage in practical planning relevant to their own classrooms. They should carry out their plans whilst the course is still in progress, if possible, and report on them to other course participants. There are many examples in this book. They include the following:

- 'I feel a whole new child' (Box 15)

- A safe and welcoming environment (Box 16)

- Reflections on parental involvement (Box 18)

- Study visit to a nursery (Box 19)

- Reflections on a welcome programme (Box 20)

- Creating systems – a consultant's story (Box 21)

- Big enough for everybody (Box 24)

- Curiosity and self-esteem (Box 32)

Figure 1 summaries a programme of professional development and review at an Oakwell secondary school. On page 50 there are extracts from focus group discussion that took place as part of the programme.

Figure 1: Review and development at one school

CHOICE OF ISSUE

The school decides to work on ways of raising the achievement of African-Caribbean students.

FOCUS GROUP

An external consultant works with a focus group of Year 8 and Year 9 students. The discussion is tape-recorded and studied by the consultant afterwards.

STAFF SEMINAR

There is a one-day seminar for senior staff.

It begins with discussion of extracts and messages from the focus group.

Staff then draw up descriptions of an ideal multicultural school. The headings are curriculum, staffing, community links, ethos, listening to pupils, policy-making.

Staff compare and contrast their real school with the ideal school.

They form action plans.

ACTION PLANS

Curriculum review

Each department will review (a) curriculum content and (b) teaching methodology, and a composite overview will be published.

Staffing

Positive action measures will be used to ensure the staff is more representative of fhe community it serves.

Ethos

Displays will be reviewed to make sure they reflect the diversity of the school.

Training

There will be staff training on pupils' perceptions and experiences.

Citizenship programme

There will be increased emphasis on giving pupils a platform and listening to their views.

Parents and community

Greater efforts will be made to communicate effectively with parents and the local community.

Box 14

Two Useful Words

When planning a training event or programme for colleagues, it is useful to have in one's mind's eye a model or map about how adults learn best. It is useful also if the model can be summarised with a memorising device so that its various component parts can easily be recalled in the right sequence.

Two possible words are A-C-T-I-O-N and A-G-E-N-D-A, as outlined below.

ACTION

A Acknowledging, accepting and affirming the experience of each individual participant, and the diversity of experience amongst participants as a group. Also, approaching agreement on the aims and agenda of the course ahead.

C Confronting complexity, controversy, contradictions, crossfire and conflict. This involves coming away from one's own comfort zones, and courting and coping with discomfort.

T Taking time to think, turning thoughts over, being tentative, testing the water.

I Introducing and investigating ideas of initiative and innovation.

O Outlining options and then opting, overtly and with openness, for particular opportunities and operations.

N Nurturing something new, and making it natural and normal.

AGENDA

An alternative mnemonic, saying much the same things, can be provided by the word A-G-E-N-D-A. In this scheme, a learning programme has three parts, signified by three pairs of letters, AG, EN and DA.

In the first part there are activities of acceptance and affirmation (A) and getting to grips with 'grievance' and 'grief' – i.e. things which are troublesome and conflictual (G).

Second, there is consideration of the experience of others, and this involves examination of case study examples (E) and taking note of notions and theories (N).

In the third and final part there is deliberation and a declaration of principles (D) and agreement on action (A).

Professional development is cyclical rather than linear. This point is nicely expressed by the word AGENDA, for the first and last letters are the same. The action with which one cycle of learning finishes is also the action which is affirmed at the start of a new cycle.

3 Listening, welcome and inclusion
– stories and experiences of pupils

Part of the community

Why are these boys in trouble so much of the time? Why is their attitude so negative? There was an anger and dismissiveness in the way they spoke, a kind of facing-up to you, a kind of 'I don't care'. We wanted to find out why. Then the Inclusive Classrooms, Inclusive Schools project arrived at just the right time, giving us the extra incentive to get moving.

With these words a teacher at Perceval Junior School in Oakwell begins her account of the school's work with a group of Somali pupils. She and her headteacher attended the inaugural conference at Oakwell Town Hall, described in Chapter 1. 'It was then,' she writes, 'that I started to think a bit more about *our* responsibility as a school for the boys' behaviour.' She continues:

> Hearing about the Lawrence family's experiences started me thinking. I wondered how the boys felt about school, and whether they felt valued, part of the community. Were we ourselves doing something that was pushing them away, making them angry and separate? Maybe, without realising it, we were part of the problem? Later when we were at the residential workshop a week or so later, the poem by James Berry [*Dreaming Black Boy*] and the activities we did made the suspicions stronger.

To investigate their suspicions further, the school arranged for a Somali member of staff to spend time with the boys they were concerned about. She wrote a description of what she had done, and her reflections about the boys and the school. Her story is shown in Box 15. It vividly shows that indeed the school had been unaware of how its Somali pupils were feeling and insensitive to the pressures that led to them being disaffected and, in the teachers' eyes, troublesome. When an adult authority figure tried to get alongside them they were at first distrustful. But their initial frostiness soon thawed when they realised that the school was genuinely interested in them and really did want to know how they were feeling. The experience of being carefully listened to made them feel far more positive about school and that they belonged. 'I feel a whole new child,' said one of them. His words are a remarkable and beautiful commendation of the project and are a fitting introduction to the rest of this chapter.

The work with a small group of boys at Perceval School, as reported in Box 15, was not one-off but was complemented by the creation of a Somali family group and a Somali home-school liaison team.

Induction and inclusion – how are we doing?

Pitshanger High School had been running an induction programme for new arrivals for a number of years. It used its grant under Oakwell's Inclusive Classrooms, Inclusive Schools (ICIS) project to assess the programme's impact and consider what improvements might need to be made. The evaluation involved interviews with 22 students who had joined the school with little or no English. Most of them were by now relatively confident speakers of English and could reflect back on their earlier experiences when they first came to the school. Most of the students interviewed were Somali. The questions for the interviews are shown in Box 17.

Extracts from the eventual report are shown in Box 16. They were fed back to all staff and had a significant influence on how newly arriving pupils are taught. They were also incorporated into the school's induction programme for new staff. Further, several of the students' remarks were displayed on a wall chart. They appreciated this and enjoyed seeing their own words reflected back to them. Their comments included:

> 'I was not sure what to do or how to behave in a lesson.'

> 'I found group work difficult.'

> 'Never in my life have I heard of RE and PSHE. 'What does that mean?' I thought.'

> 'Everything seemed strange to me. I couldn't understand why everyone went to a different room for each subject.'

> 'I had no idea what lesson I was in.'

> 'I thought this was a mad lesson.' (Said of a drama lesson in which pupils were being required to hit each other!)

> 'I couldn't understand a thing. I didn't have a clue what the teacher was talking about.'

Box 15

I feel a whole new child

A Somali member of staff describes her work with a group of Somali boys

At first the boys felt left out, no one was listening to them, the whole school was against them.

Yusuf

Yusuf was always getting into trouble with teachers, dinner people and other staff. For that particular day he was sent home for pushing a dinner lady. When he came back the next day he said it is always me who gets the blame, it seems no one is listening, no one wants to know us, why are we different? Just because I am always in trouble that doesn't mean I did it.

Saed

Saed decided to go to the park one day instead of the school. When I asked why, he said no one cares. I am always doing things wrong – my teacher will be happy if I am not around, so will the other children.

So he spends the day in the park under a tree and on that day it was raining heavily and also very cold. He went home at normal time so no one would suspect he didn't go to school. He told me he found it difficult to make friends, he had no friends at school, and education wasn't his priority.

Mohammed

Deep down, Mohammed was a lonely child. He spent his time after school wandering around town. He knew that if he hung around with Abdul he would be noticed. He always had money and he would buy things for the other children, so he could win their friendship.

Abdul

Abdul was popular with his classmates – the whole school knew who Abdul was. He was often in trouble and outside his classroom. He seemed to enjoy winding up staff and other children. In spite of all of this he was a likeable child, who would sometimes try to do the right thing but would often fail to keep the effort up. He needed to be rewarded for every little task.

What I did

I have worked with the boys individually and in groups to talk about school and home life. At first they were reluctant to talk to me about their problems. They needed to ask me questions about my life. In one of the sessions we talked about life in Somalia and what they can remember. Most of the boys were too young when the war broke but older children had told them about families and friends lost during the war. I personally found it difficult to talk about the war with the boys, it brought back memories and un-dealt-with emotions. They said to me it is OK to talk about things that are difficult, we have all been through the war and talking about it will help all of us deal with it.

But as they got to know me in person they started to open up. Their attitudes about learning and school in general were becoming positive. They started contributing to the lessons and getting involved in other curricular activities. They talked about exam results and their achievements in class. They became more confident in speaking Somali and meeting once a week helped their communication skills, self-esteem and confidence. They also discussed their feelings and how they can help each other and set examples to the younger children in the school.

Creating a display

Somali boys and girls in years 5 and 6 spent time on the Internet researching and making a display for the corridor about their culture. Some of them brought in pictures and clothes from home to show. After this they felt that staff and other children were valuing their culture and beliefs. "We feel we are part of the school. People are listening and teachers are making time to help us with our work." They started talking to the other children about life in Somalia.

'A whole new child'

One child said," I feel a whole new child". Another said," I might look different outside but I am same inside. All it needs is time and understanding from the school to know the cultural differences."

Box 16

A safe and welcoming environment

Interviews with 22 recently arrived students revealed that:

Without exception they found the school to be a safe and welcoming environment.

In 21 out of 22 cases the school's 'buddy system' had turned out to be successful. One student said. "About six people helped me on my first day. I felt happy and good. Suddenly my feelings about being nervous went."

Without exception, students found the induction programme helpful. They felt safe and more confident than in mainstream classrooms about talking in front of others. They enjoyed being with other new arrivals and learning about other languages, cultures, countries and religions. All the students interviewed believed it gave them a sense of confidence as well as an understanding of how the school works.

Students found the issue of where to sit initially quite problematic. They would have preferred teachers to tell them in the first instance where to sit. Some relied on the teacher to indicate where they should sit whilst others relied on their buddy to direct them to a seat. Some had no idea at all of where to sit.

Some students said that they found it comforting when teachers asked them their names and introduced themselves. One girl commented how good she felt when a teacher told her what a lovely name she had. Another student cited a teacher who asked him about his country of origin and his language and he went on to explain how pleased he was that a teacher showed an interest in him.

In terms of how students followed the lessons, we have learnt a lot about what strategies they found particularly helpful in their first few weeks. They mentioned the use of visual aids and gestures as being especially helpful. Teachers who explained individually to students made it easier for them, and support teachers were named as being of enormous help.

Students employed strategies such as looking for similarities in their own language, getting their buddies to translate and using bilingual dictionaries. The interviewees spoke of other useful strategies such as translating basic subject-specific vocabulary into different languages, differentiated work, having translations of useful phrases, drawing pictures, support in their home language, dictionaries in the classroom and being placed with good role models who speak the same language at home. Some students mentioned how helpful it was when at the end of the first few lessons the teachers asked how they had coped and told them not to worry. Students were pleased when homework was explained to them individually by the subject teacher or the support teacher.

Students appreciated the introduction cards given to them in case they became lost or had a problem and were unable to express themselves.

As part of the school's induction programme for new staff, we have been able to use the findings of the interviews to encourage good practice in the future.

We have learnt how simple things such as the teachers introducing themselves, guiding the pupil to his or her seat in that first lesson, making a positive comment to the pupil, giving him or her tasks such as handing out the books, making classrooms reflect the subject better, referring to the student's language or country and sometimes just smiling can change that nervous child into one who looks forward to returning the next day.

What has been particularly interesting about this project is how much we have been able to learn about the feelings of new arrivals, and how some simple practices can so strongly affect how a new arrival perceives their new school.

The questions used in the interviews are shown in Box 17 overleaf.

Box 17

First days at this school

1. Think back to your first few days here. How did you feel?

2. What did we do to help you on your first day?

3. Did you feel safe? Did you feel welcome? Explain.

4. Were you given a friend or buddy to help you?

5. How did other pupils treat you? Were they helpful?

6. Were there times when you felt alone or lost?

7. Did you know what lessons you were in?

8. Did you know where to sit?

9. Did teachers know you were new? Did they know your name?

10. Looking back, what would have made things easier for you in your first few weeks?

11. Is there anything that has made it difficult for you to learn?

12. Since arriving, what do you think has helped your English to improve?

13. Do you have help with your English at home?

14. Do you think we recognised the skills and knowledge you had before you came here?

15. What do you think are the biggest problems for Somali refugees settling in (a) at this school and (b) in the UK?

16. If you could improve one thing for new arrivals what would you suggest?

Source: interview schedule at Pitshanger High School

Involvement of parents

In one of the projects funded under the ICIS programme, training materials were compiled on how Oakwell nursery schools involve parents in the curriculum. Staff made a pack containing five modules.

Module One set out the underlying philosophy, the importance staff attach to genuine parental involvement, and the empowering of parents by giving them understanding of the issues and of how they can help to teach their children.

Module Two was about the things parents can do at home to teach their children to read. It included a book lending scheme and an outline plan for workshops.

Module Three was about using storybags to develop literacy and numeracy skills. It included photographic examples of the resources and resource cards, with examples of supporting non-fiction and extension activities.

Module Four was a mathematics resource pack that brought together games made by parents to support their children's mathematical development in the nursery and at home.

Module Five outlined the aims of a teddy bear project, organised to build and develop home school links by involving parents in the curriculum for personal and social development.

Staff reflections on the project are shown in Box 18.

Reviewing and improving EAL

Early years staff at Chaplin Primary School were aware that they were not as up to date as they needed to be with the theory and practice of helping children to learn English as an additional language. They used their grant under the ICIS programme to arrange a study visit for them all to visit a beacon school on the other side of London, and then to fund a consultant to help them reflect on what they observed on the visit, and to develop suitable methods and materials for use with the children. Box 19 contains an extract from the ensuing report.

It is clear that the journey itself to another area of the city, as also the experience of being warmly welcomed at the end of the journey, were important components of the total event. The point is obvious, but nevertheless worth highlighting – study visits, even modest events taking up no more than an afternoon, can be invaluable for acquainting teachers with new ideas. The ideas gained on a visit are not necessarily any better than those presented in a talk or lecture. But they are likely to make a deeper impression and so are more likely to be remembered and acted on.

Welcome programme at Key Stage 1

Cleveland Primary School set up an induction programme for new arrivals at KS1. A classroom was set aside where the activities took place. The resources included a home-corner, painting, sand, water areas and a construction area, and also books, games, puzzles and a computer. The programme consisted of 16 sessions, two hours a week for eight weeks. The children were withdrawn from different classes for these sessions. There were twelve children in the programme, with their origins in Kosovo, Iraq, Pakistan, India and Ghana. The children were divided into three groups of four and the groups rotated between the different activities.

Every lesson started with teacher and children introducing themselves to each other, saying their name, country, class and class teacher's name. A short session of mental maths, which included learning number rhymes, was followed by table activities and story time on the carpet. The stories fitted in with the topic of the session – school, myself, and so on. So far as possible other children came as well, to play with the children in the induction programme and to give models for English and help form friendships.

The teacher responsible for the programme was subsequently interviewed about it. The questions included: why? how did it go? what was the impact on race equality? what was the impact on the school as a whole? what did you learn? what would you or will you do differently another time? what advice and warnings would you have for anyone embarking on a similar project in another school? Her answers are shown in Box 20.

Box 18

Reflections on parental involvement

We now feel that we can use the pack as a basis for training in early years and primary settings. We need, though, to think about how the inset can be organised most effectively, so that it's relevant to individual schools.

We think the pack makes a genuine contribution to improving the access and involvement of children and parents in the curriculum. In this sense it has an important contribution to make to issues of race equality, particularly when children and families are targeted properly.

Other staff in the nurseries are beginning to become aware of the content of the modules through inset/training days, although the issue of access still needs to be more widely discussed and disseminated.

There is a need to make it clear to parents at the outset, on their child's home visit, that their involvement is essential and expected. Parents need to know that they share responsibility with us for their child's education and to understand the need to make a commitment of their time both in the classroom and at home.

Parent workshops and staff inset need to be planned in from the start of the school year, so that they are an integral part of the school year. These need to be responsive to and reflect the needs of particular parent groups and their children.

Box 19

Study visit to a nursery

We set off early one morning to brave the journey to North Islington. We made good time and found the nursery easily. As we went into the nursery we immediately felt very welcome and were greeted by the headteacher. She told us about the nursery, how it evolved into what it is today and how it is organised and run. We were introduced to the idea of 'core texts'. These are a set of books (at least twenty) which are used extensively and revisited frequently during the year. A core text must have a good story structure and repetitive language with illustrations which excite and hold the children's interest. With each text there are sets of games, story props, dressing up clothes and story tapes in different languages.

We were given examples of planning and assessment, and then there was a guided tour of the nursery. After the tour we were given the opportunity to explore the nursery in our own time. This was invaluable, for we made observations of many examples of good practice, both in the delivery of the curriculum and in the organisation of resources and learning areas. We had the opportunity at the end of our visit to ask the head questions about what we had seen during the visit. It was so inspiring to see such good early years practice that some of us decided to attend a whole day Saturday workshop at the nursery a few weeks later. We worked with a specific text, *Peace at Last* by Jill Murphy, and were shown how to make activities and games to develop language, maths and literacy. The principles can easily be transferred to other core texts.

Two days later the consultant came to run a workshop for us. He had a quick look around the early years classrooms and he looked at our planning and some of the resources we had already made, and gave us feedback. He also took us through the principles behind how children learn an additional language, taken from the research carried out by Jim Cummins in Canada. Before he came into school, we talked about some issues that we wanted to discuss.

We learned about the importance of valuing what the children already know. We also learned the importance of introducing new texts in a variety of ways to make the text accessible to the children. For example, when planning to read *Mrs Wishy Washy*, we can set up in advance various activities that introduce objects and language which feature in the text – a wash day with a washing line and bath tub, etc.

It is also important that children learning an additional language are provided with cognitively demanding work, and they need key visuals to support their thinking and lead them into enquiry. We can prepare story props and games which encourage and organise children's thinking. We found out that it is particularly important that children should have plenty of opportunities to use interactive and collaborative language based on structured exercises and activities. These are best catered for in mixed ability collaborative group work.

We learned that it is also important to provide opportunities for children to use their first language. We have bought and made more bilingual books and tapes and have more bilingual support in the classrooms. By displaying different scripts we value the home languages of the children more than we did before. We have improved our provision for an increasing number of children from diverse communities joining our school.

Next term we are going to set up workshops for parents to develop story props and bilingual tapes.

If we had the opportunity to do another project in the future, we would organise a whole day workshop for all staff. It would include a balance of theory and practice and provide opportunities for teachers to make resources to be used in the classroom.

Box 20

Reflections on a welcome programme

Why?

The school had a high percentage of newly arrived children in both KS1 and 2. All the children came with little or no English and some had experienced traumatic events. Adrian and Afrim, two brothers from Kosovo, were initially very disturbed. They cried and did not want to go to the classroom. It was felt that this programme would ease the settling-in process and meet the children's emotional needs. The children were given time and space to explore their emotions through painting and drawing. Some started off drawing aeroplanes and bombs falling from the sky. It was interesting to see how the children's drawings and paintings changed over time from dark, sombre colour themes to brighter and altogether happier moods and themes and they were happy to talk about their lives here and now.

How did it go?

The programme has been very successful in supporting the settling-in process. Class teachers have noticed a marked improvement in the children's confidence in the classroom. One day there was a supply teacher in one class. When she asked the children to introduce themselves, the children on the induction programme were the first ones to do so. The other children in the class were more reluctant.

At the end of the eight weeks some children were ready to move on to more curriculum related work; the others stayed in the induction programme but were given more complex tasks.

What is the impact on race equality?

Staff in the school have gained much background knowledge about the children as individuals but also about their difference cultures. This has improved staff attitudes to the children. Some teachers have wanted to learn how to say hello and thank you in different languages to help the children feel accepted in the classroom. It has also helped the class teachers to have higher expectations of what the children are able to do.

Parents were invited to weekly coffee mornings where they could also ask questions and be given information about school issues. They have felt really welcome and empowered. Some parents have been encouraged to help in a class and felt happy to do so. They are now able to support their children at home in a much more informed way. Many parents have been surprised to know how much a child can learn through play and how helpful it is to a child if parents read and tell stories in their own languages.

What has been the impact on the school as a whole?

The staff are more confident in dealing with children of many different nationalities, languages, religions and customs. The headteacher has been a keen supporter of the two induction programmes.

What have you learnt?

To have an organised induction programme even for KS1 has benefited the children, the class teachers and the whole school. When we see children like Adrian, Afrim, Iyvan and Shain joining in class discussions, who were all so shy beforehand, we know this has been worthwhile.

What would you or will you do differently another time?

We would like to involve more confident English speaking children to come and play and talk to the new-comers.

What advice and warnings would you have for anyone embarking on a similar project in another school?

Do not hesitate to set up a KS1 induction programme. It is well worth the effort. The cost can be kept down by getting resources from the classes whose children are attending the programme. Could some of your EMAG allocation go towards this? Warning: Please note that the programme is for a specific length of time only.

If possible try to involve the parents of the newly arrived children by setting up regular meetings with them, where you can explain things and they can ask questions and build up a network of friends and help break their isolation.

Box 21

Creating systems — a consultant's story

The problem

I was asked to develop and support the EMAG work in two schools in Oakwell. In both there was limited specialist provision for raising achievement of pupils from minority ethnic backgrounds, which meant there was:

- no clear action plan for the development and focus of EMAG work
- no systems for identification and assessment of level of English language development
- a lack of specific information on children that could inform EMAG-focused work
- no programme to support new arrivals
- no EMAG Policy
- the EMAG-funded staff saw the focus of their work as supporting class teachers rather than raising the achievement of the children.

The task

My role was to create systems that would support the development of all staff – mainstream and EMAG-funded – to ensure that all pupils received their rightful entitlement to education. I realised very early on that to create something robust and effective it had to be embedded in whole-school practice, so the process was as important as, if not more important than, the end product. If the process were not inclusive the systems would not be sustained after I left.

In each school the deputy head, the EMAG-funded staff and I looked at what was working and what was not. We talked with all members of staff, ensuring their input was valued and appreciated. Through this evaluation we identified what we needed to create:

- clear systems to track and monitor the language development of pupils learning English as an additional language
- systems to gather clear and comprehensive background information
- a welcome pack for new families and a programme for new children
- class resources to support collaborative, interactive classrooms
- whole-school, one-to-one and team training to raise achievement of pupils from minority ethnic backgrounds, including those learning English as an additional language.

Targets

Following the identification of need the next step was to break down each area into 'bite-sized' pieces. At such times I always imagine myself being on a road. Behind me there are situations where there are limited systems to support pupils and ahead of me are good, robust, clear systems that support pupils effectively. I am between these two places. So long as I take steps towards my goal that is fine, no matter how small the steps. Just so long as I am not taking steps backwards!

Action plans

The first item in the action plans was a policy for teaching English as an additional language. We developed this together. The systems and processes included:

- a pupil profile which paid particular attention to assessing and monitoring English language development
- developing assessment using the QCA extended scale processes for monitoring English language development
- an initial assessment for new arrivals, pupils returning after an extended leave of more that half a term and pupils who were to receive specialist support or focus from EMAG-funded staff
- a system to monitor progress

In-house interpreting service

In both schools initiated an 'in house' interpreting service. We asked mid-day meal supervisors, cooks, cleaners, learning support assistants and teachers what languages they spoke, read and wrote besides English. We collated this information and then circulated the results. It was now possible to support parents with interpretation far more effectively than before.

What did I learn?

While working in the two schools in Oakwell I learnt a great deal, the most poignant being the importance of having clarity about the direction in which we wished to go and then working creatively together to get there. Working as a team makes the kind of huge difference that an individual on their own can make only with struggle and difficulty. The teams in the two schools varied and included any combination of myself, the class teacher, the EMAG-funded staff and the whole staff. The systems that were initiated in both schools are able to work effectively because they were initiated and developed by a school team and embedded in whole-school practice.

As EMAG-funded staff we work with some of the most vulnerable children in a school. Many of the children we work with will go to their family's country of origin at some point in their lives, whether for a holiday or to live permanently. They may move on through re-housing, and may be with us for only a few months. If we work to create a passion for learning, and classrooms and schools that work for everyone and have no one left out, and if we celebrate win/win approaches to life, then the children will carry that with them in their hearts and take it wherever they go in the world.

Rethinking provision for raising achievement

At the time of the ICIS project there were two schools in Oakwell which, due to recent staff resignations, had only limited specialist provision for English as an additional language, The LEA advised them to respond to their situation creatively by using their EMAG funds to set up patterns of excellent practice. Rather than immediately recruiting teachers or bilingual classroom assistants, the schools spent the money over two terms to pay for a consultant to work with them for one or two days a week. The consultant would:

* involve the school staff in setting up systems suitable for the school

* give professional development and training to the staff in using them.

Once the systems were in place, the schools recruited staff. It was invaluable that there was by now a strong infrastructure, owned and used by the whole staff. In due course the consultant was asked to write an account of her contributions to the two schools. Her story is shown in Box 21.

The consultant who wrote the story in Box 21 mentions the value of providing simple but reliable advice in an accessible form for mainstream colleagues. Box 22 shows an extract from such advice.

All the stories in this chapter have been about the importance of high expectations. The next chapter contains an extended discussion of the concept of expectation, and is illustrated by a further substantial story from an Oakwell School.

Box 22

Pupils new to English

Points to remember

- Pupils learning English as an additional language are not a homogeneous group

- They do have a language to build on

- They want to communicate and therefore must be treated as communicators

- They need to be able to ask questions – give them the grammar, the conventions and the confidence

- Language learning takes place with and through other learning

- Emphasis should be on meaning rather than on form

- Listening is a part of the language learning process

- But too much listening, without opportunities to respond and interact, is stressful

- We must plan to ensure that pupils have experiences of success

- Language is extended and developed through being exposed to a range of situations, contexts and language models

- Learning a language is a creative, risk-taking process that inevitably involves making errors and requires understanding rules, so the environment must be supportive

- Learning a language is not a linear process

- Basic information must be available to us about the language background and language behaviour of our pupils

- Bilingualism is a special achievement. It is educationally enriching, has positive effects on intellectual performance and is of immense value both to individuals and to society

Source: various Oakwell schools

4 Great Expectations
– desiring and intending the best for all

We hope and intend

'The school is damp-proofed,' say the staff at Broadway Primary School, 'and underpinned, burglar-alarmed, double-glazed and insulated. We hope that it's a place of safety where the real world can be examined under bright learning lights and where children can be supported in developing coping strategies for what they will and do face out there. And we hope and intend that it should be big enough to fit everybody in!' In the fuller story (Box 24) from which this is an extract it is clear that the references to the school building are metaphors. Damp-proofing, for example, is a metaphor for keeping out unhelpful ideas and assumptions that might otherwise seep in.

The school's story is a vivid introduction to the themes of this chapter. It starts by recalling the programme in Oakwell of which it is a part, and the inaugural conference which started everything off. It then describes how the school set about reviewing its values and policies. One aspect of the review was a one-day conference for all staff, both teaching and administrative. The day contained several of the exercises and activities that were described in Chapter 2.

Against the background of this review, the school resolved to renew and reinforce its longstanding involvement with another LEA-level initiative in Oakwell, to do with learning styles and accelerated learning. Staff felt that certain pupils were under-achieving in the sense that they were not reaching their potential, even though they were doing well in relation to national and local norms. Uncertain how to proceed, however, they began by consulting one pupil – rather in the same way that the school cited in Box 15 ('I feel a whole new child') began by approaching and listening to a specific pupil. The initial interview was not long, but was more than enough to encourage staff to feel they were on to something of substantial importance.

After the story in Box 24, the chapter pulls back to recall the concept of teacher expectations. Significant research on the concept dates from the 1960s, particularly in the United States, but the idea that a person's behaviour is crucially affected by what other people perceive and anticipate goes back much further. To recall this point, the chapter uses some quotations from the novel by Charles Dickens whose title is also the chapter's title. The chapter then outlines some of the work done in Oakwell on accelerated learning and learning style theory. It closes by discussing the ways in which learning style theory needs to be integrated with explicitly antiracist perspectives.

The crucial importance of high expectations is stressed in the extract in Box 23.

Box 23

Her expectations were high

If it hadn't been for the sensitivity, insight and superhuman patience of one of my teachers, I don't know what my fate would have been. While other teachers gave up on me when it became clear that I had given up on them, she took the trouble to look beyond my dilated pupils and sense that there was someone in there desperate to achieve at something of real, three-dimensional value. So where others retreated from me in a mirror image of my retreat from them, she came closer, giving me more and more responsibilities, challenges and status. Her expectations were high and it was her belief in my ability to meet those expectations in the end that motivated me not only to hang in there but to shine.

Reva Klein, *Defying Disaffection*, Trentham Books, 1999

Nin waliba maalintuu dhashaa kitaab qoorta loo sudhaa oo la yidha haa, "Laguma dhaamee dhaqaaq."

On the day that every child is born a label should be dangled from their neck "Walk tall: no one is better than you."

Somali saying contributed by a teacher at one of the Oakwell workshops

Box 24

Big enough to fit everybody in – one school's journey

Taking stock

When the Inclusive Classrooms, Inclusive Schools information came into the school we were really excited. The fundamental commitment of the school is to ensure each individual will succeed and feel good about himself/herself. We recognised at once that the ICIS project was all about what we believed we were about. Three of us attended the Town Hall conference and were energised. The messages we heard were in keeping with what we believed. We wanted to embark on a project. What was it to be?

First, we had to take stock. The conference emphasis on the Stephen Lawrence Inquiry made us re-look at important issues, not least because the debate about the education of black children has been removed from the government agenda. It has been replaced by a concern for a centrally controlled and uniformly delivered primary curriculum. The findings of the Macpherson Report brought back into focus the dangerously unchallenged beliefs of racial superiority and hostility that are endemic in our society and formalised in the systems of our institutions. We were reminded at the conference that the children who walked to our school each morning and home again at night are prey to these prejudices. We were realistic enough to know that the prejudices are apparent in our own school, seeping between the foundation stones.

So one of the first things we had to do was take another look at our foundation stones, our fundamental beliefs in inclusion, equality and respect. Renewing the foundations, that was what was needed. Otherwise we'd just be papering over the cracks.

Agenda and context

We started by organising a day conference for the whole staff, including all admin and support staff, and for as many governors as could make it. It was on the first training day back after the summer holiday – a signal of its importance! It was run for us by the same person who

had run the borough conference at the Town Hall. It challenged all of us to recognise in ourselves cultural stories, and we received understandings about others and ourselves. These stories are how we construct our national identity and decide who shares this identity with us. We took part in a carousel of ingenious activities told us about London and about our school population. We read challenging material from the media that reinforced the notion that only a few of us naturally belong and are welcome members of society.

The experience was troubling, stimulating and challenging. But we had an agenda for our next move. The foundation stones had been re-sunk, re-grouted and re-defined. In consequence our damp-proofing – the school's antiracist policy – would be all the more effective.

We also had to clear out the attic, the place where outdated ideas, stereotypes and suspicions are stored, should they ever be needed. For example, those ideas of the 1960s which allowed black people to be pushed aside as unlikely to succeed or have a contribution to make. People were bussed, assessed, mistrusted, misunderstood, misinterpreted, misdirected, suspected, rejected and excluded. All these things hadn't been thrown away, but were gathering dust in the attic and the dust was falling through cracks in the ceiling. If we are not vigilant, the dust from outdated history dulls our bright new understanding!

I can almost hear you musing that we've talked about the foundations, the damp proofing and the attic. So where are the bricks and mortar? The fabric of the building is the inclusive curriculum. The bricks are the identities, contributions, achievements, cultures and journeys of all the members of the school community. They are cemented by an acceptance of difference and an understanding that we can all learn from each other. The walls have ears: they're listening to each other's stories!

And there are windows – we all need natural light. The windows represent our need as adults and children to reflect on what is happening inside our school, and to see

Box 24 continued

what's going on outside too. And there's the artificial light – extra lighting provided by the school. This is our commitment to empowering children, helping them to switch on their own learning lights, not only for today but also as an investment in their futures and ours.

African-Caribbean achievement

So this was the context in which we planned a project around African-Caribbean achievement. We chose this topic not because our African-Caribbean pupils are underachieving, for they are not, or not in comparison with the school average or the LEA average. But we were aware that African-Caribbean achievement is an issue in London and England generally, and we were pretty sure that our school was not stretching all our black pupils intellectually, and was in that sense failing them. In particular we were anxious about the fact that we seemed to be failing the black boys at our school with regard to mathematics.

But what should we actually do? We were totally sure we didn't want to work with a deficit model, the notion that there was something wrong with the pupils themselves or with their community. But knowing what you don't want isn't the same as knowing what you do want. What, to repeat, should we do?

What we did is obvious enough in retrospect, but at the time it seemed quite a new departure – we decided to ask the children! For many years the school had been interested in, and committed to, effective and accelerated learning, and most staff applied learning style theory in their teaching, ensuring a mix of visual, auditory and kinaesthetic (VAC) activities. But we had tended to be colour-blind. We hadn't used learning style theory within an explicitly antiracist framework.

Interview

We began by interviewing one boy, let's call him Paul. If Paul was amazed to be invited to the head's study and to be asked a series of peculiar questions by the head and deputy head, he didn't show it. On the contrary, he was clearly delighted that we were taking such a close interest in him and in the ways he learns things and how his mind works. 'We're not talking to you because you're doing badly in maths,' we said. 'The fact is, you're doing quite well. But we think you could do better. We're talking to you because we want you to help us help you.' Much of the ensuing interview was about how Paul had learnt from his mother and sister how to fry eggs! The interview had a very positive effect on Paul himself and was valuable for this reason alone – the time and effort we put into it would have been justified even if we hadn't gone any further.

But we did go further. We talked to Paul's class teacher and were able to give a lot of focused guidance on what Paul would and wouldn't find valuable. For example, it was clear that visual activities were very important for him but that problem-solving through talking with other pupils was not something that was going to help him. We followed this up, and in our next interview with him we asked him to tell us about something he had recently learnt in maths, and what had helped him. Later we worked with other pupils, both as individuals and in groups, using the model interview that we had first developed with Paul.

Journeys

Our theme for Black History Month was 'Journeys'. Literally, journeys from one part of the world to another. But mental journeys too. And we were aware that our school is on a journey. It hasn't reached its goal.

The school is damp-proofed, underpinned, burglar-alarmed, double-glazed and insulated. We hope that it's a place of safety where the real world can be examined under bright learning lights and where children can be supported in developing coping strategies for what they will and do face out there.

And we hope and intend that it should be big enough to fit everybody in!

What schools and societies expect

In her best-selling autobiography *Bad Blood* Lorna Sage recalls the rural primary school she attended in the late 1940s. Basically, she says, the assumption was that the role of schools is 'to reflect your ready-made place in the scheme of things and put you firmly back where you came from'. One day, the headteacher lined up the senior class and went along the line predicting for each child their future occupation in life: 'You'll be a muck-shoveller, you'll be a muck-shoveller ...' He spoke these words, says Sage, with 'gloomy satisfaction'.

Twenty-five years later, Lee Jasper was at school in Oldham. Recalling his time there, he wrote later:

> Education was typical of the attitudes of the time: the posh kids got all the attention. Those from the poorest sections of the white working class, British-born blacks, those from the Caribbean (particularly the boys) and the Bangladeshis were all in the bottom class ... The teachers were in the main ex-grammar-school unreconstructed racists. That they were forced to teach black and Asian children was an insult to both their professional standing and the notion of Empire. They made their distaste known by the expression of their extreme prejudice. They simply refused to teach us.

Nowadays, no teacher or headteacher would communicate low expectations of their pupils with such bluntness or cruelty as did Lorna Sage's headteacher. And few if any teachers nowadays are 'ex-grammar-school unreconstructed racists'. It is still the case, however, that society has its hierarchies, pecking orders and notions of what is posh, and that these affect the expectations teachers have of their pupils, and the expectations pupils have of themselves. Also it is still the case that many Asian and black people are on the lowest rungs of society's various ladders, and that they will not move higher unless and until they and their teachers have higher expectations than those which currently prevail. Further, it is still the case that high and low expectations are communicated to pupils both directly by what teachers say and indirectly through how teachers behave, and that expectations can be self-fulfilling prophesies. As for understandings of British history and Empire, these too still need to be addressed. There is fuller discussion of them in Chapters 5 and 6.

Not that teacher expectations are only or even primarily about life-chances and employment in the distant future. They are also about things that may happen later today, or even in the next hour or minute. And they are often much more to do with pupils' behaviour than with their academic attainment. These points are mentioned in Box 24 and have been put well in a newspaper article by the leader of a teachers' union. He writes: 'This morning many teachers will go to school dreading the prospect of facing a particular class. It could be a class with which last week's lesson went particularly badly, a class where almost every lesson goes badly, or a group with one individual who cannot keep still or keep quiet for more than a few minutes at a time.' There is a longer quotation from his article in Box 26.

My father's name being Pirrip

It is interesting to recall the ways in which the central character of *Great Expectations* by Charles Dickens is affected by other people's perceptions and predictions. The opening paragraph of the novel proclaims a rugged and assertive independence: 'My father's name being Pirrip and my Christian name Philip, my infant tongue could make of both names nothing longer or more explicit than Pip. So I called myself Pip, and came to be called Pip.' But Pip's capacity to define himself and his surrounding reality does not last. The novel as a whole is about his confrontation with other people's expectations and perceptions and his continual adjustments and negotiations as he interacts with others. There are several quotations on these themes in Box 25.

One of the quotations in Box 25 recalls Pip's first realisation that he belongs to a particular level in society's pecking order – 'a stupid, clumsy labouring boy' – and describes how he acts out the physical and manual clumsiness that is expected of him. There is a similar reference to social status, as also to gender, in the passage when someone says sternly to Pip: 'I have a pretty large experience of boys, and you're a bad set of fellows.' Much later in the novel Pip's good friend Herbert Pockett gives him substantial affirmation by refusing to summarise him or pigeonhole him in an over-simplifying way: 'A good fellow, with impetuosity and hesitation, boldness and diffidence, action and dreaming, curiously mixed in him.'

Box 25

Expectations small and great

Stupid, clumsy labouring boy

"He calls the knaves Jacks, this boy!" said Estella with disdain, before our first game was out. "And what coarse hands he has. And what thick boots!" I had never thought of being ashamed of my hands before; but I began to consider them a very indifferent pair. Her contempt was so strong that it became infectious, and I caught it. She won the game, and I dealt. I misdealt, as was only natural, when I knew she was lying in wait for me to do wrong; and she denounced me for a stupid, clumsy labouring boy. (Chapter 8)

They always begin by asking questions

"Please, what's Hulks?" said I. "That's the way with this boy!" exclaimed my sister, pointing me out with her needle and thread, and shaking her head at me. "Answer him one question, and he'll ask you a dozen directly. Hulks are prison ships..." – "I wonder who's put into prison-ships, and why they're put there?" said I. It was too much for her. "I tell you what, young fellow," said she. "I didn't bring you up to badger people's lives out... People are put in the Hulks because they do murder, and because they rob, and forge, and do all sorts of bad; and they always begin by asking questions. Now, you get along to bed!" (Chapter 2)

Nothing so finely perceived and felt

In the little world in which children have their existence, there is nothing so finely perceived and so finely felt as injustice. It may be only small injustice that the child can be exposed to; but the child is small, and its world is small, and its rocking-horse stands as many hands high, according to scale, as a big-boned Irish hunter. (Chapter 8)

Whom have we here?

"Whom have we here?" asked the gentleman, stopping and looking at me. "A boy," said Estella. "Boy of the neighbourhood? Hey?" said he. "Yes, sir," said I. "Well! Behave yourself. I have a pretty large experience of boys, and you're a bad set of fellows. Now mind!" said he, biting the side of his great forefinger as he frowned at me, "you behave yourself!" (Chapter 11)

Curiously mixed

"You call me a lucky fellow," said I. "Of course I am. I was a blacksmith's boy but yesterday; I am – what shall I say I am? – today?" Herbert replied: "Say, a good fellow, if you want a phrase," smiling and clapping his hand on the back of mine. "A good fellow, with impetuosity and hesitation, boldness and diffidence, action and dreaming, curiously mixed in him." I stopped for a moment to consider whether there really was this mixture in my character. On the whole, I by no means recognised the analysis, but thought it not worth disputing. (Chapter 31)

Had been in me

We owed so much to Herbert's ever cheerful industry and readiness that I often wondered how I had conceived that old idea of his ineptitude, until I was one day enlightened by the reflection that perhaps the ineptitude had never been in him at all, but had been in me. (Chapter 58)

Great Expectations by Charles Dickens was first published in 1861.

Some of these extracts have been very slightly edited, to make them clearer out of context.

To be seen as 'a complex mixture' is to be seen justly. But to be seen as a mere category ('labouring boy', or indeed just 'boy') is to be perceived and treated unjustly. 'In the little world in which children have their existence,' remarks the adult Pip looking back on his childhood, 'there is nothing so finely perceived and so finely felt as injustice. It may be only small injustice that the child can be exposed to; but the child is small, and its world is small, and its rocking-horse stands as many hands high, according to scale, as a big-boned Irish hunter.' It is alas not uncommon for children and young people to feel unjustly treated by their teachers – see, for example, the quotations in Box 9 in the previous chapter, 'How it was at school'.

The fragments from *Great Expectations* in Box 25 help pose essential questions for schools. What are the expectations we have of our pupils? How do we communicate these expectations? Do our expectations in any way hinder, constrict or stifle the pupils? Or do they release them, bring out the best in them? Do we see them as 'mixtures' or as simplified categories? To what extent are our expectations influenced by social class, gender, race, ethnicity and culture? Do our pupils have a sense of justice? Or of injustice? How do the pupils see us their teachers? Do they get from us the message that we expect great things of them, both now today and also in their future lives?

Mental maps

To begin answering and handling these questions, it is valuable to use the concept of 'mental map' or 'mental model'. Also, it is relevant to explore the word 'expect'. There are connotations of seeing – one forms a picture in one's mind's eye of a future occurrence or situation. One does this in order to be prepared, wise before the event. One's expectations are weapons in one's armoury, as one goes forwards into an uncertain and possibly risky future. For to be forewarned is to be forearmed – expecting rain, one carries an umbrella. The word 'expect' also has connotations of uncertainty ('assume', 'imagine', 'suppose', are often close synonyms) and sometimes implies risk-taking and bargaining.

A bit of a mess of things

I taught Stephen for two good years in all. One episode springs to mind... Stephen could be really stubborn and so could I. One day, quite out of character, he handed in some awful, shoddy work. I knew from past experience that he could do one hundred per cent better.

'Go and do this properly, Stephen,' I said.

Stephen stood staring at the awful piece of work.

'Did you hear me?' I said.

Stephen didn't budge.

'If you don't take this away and do it properly, I shall tear it up,' I threatened.

Stephen still didn't budge.

At this point, I was aware that I should not have made that threat. I was wrong, but I thought I had to be consistent. I didn't want to lose face, so I tore up his work.

I never expected Stephen to stand up to me. We were both wrong. Stephen went home angry and upset.

Doreen, his mother, was working at the school at that time. She came to see me and we sorted it out together. I apologised. Stephen did too. We agreed that we had both made a bit of a mess of things.

Stephen was a good lad. We must make sure that we help all our children learn to live in peace. What happened to Stephen must never happen again.

Source: *The Life of Stephen Lawrence* by Verna Allette Wilkins. The teacher telling this story was Mr Gladwell, Eglington Junior School. There is fuller information about *The Life of Stephen Lawrence* in Chapter 6.

What's in a word?

Expect, v.t. Look forward to, wait, wait for; regard as likely, (I expect her to come), assume as a future event or occurrence; look for in anticipation; look for as appropriate or one's due (I expect co-operation, expect you to be here, expected better of you); think, suppose (I expect we'll be on time). From Latin *ex* (going out, going forth) + *spectare*, look, and specere, see, behold (cf spectacle, spectre, aspect, inspect, suspect, circumspect, prospect, spy, conspicuous, spectrum).

Synonyms: assume, believe, calculate, conjecture, forecast, foresee, imagine, predict, reckon, speculate, suppose, surmise, think, trust; anticipate, await, bargain for, contemplate, envisage, hope for, look ahead to, look for, look forward to, watch for; count on, demand, insist on, rely on, require, want, wish.

Source: *Oxford Dictionary of English Etymology* 1966 and *Collins Thesaurus* 1984

The picture of possibilities in one's mind's eye has two aspects. First and more obviously, there is an image of something *specific* – rain, say. But also, deeper down, there is an image of diversity and therefore of general possibilities – just at the moment I am expecting rain but I am aware that the climate is diverse. Sometimes there is hot sunlight, sometimes wind, sometimes snow, and so on. The map of *general* possibilities in one's mind's eye is the basis on which *particular expectations* are formed. The distinction between mental map and specific predictions can be readily applied in education. One the one hand, there is an overall map of general possibilities. On the other, there are expectations of one particular pupil or group of pupils.

One obvious continuum in the mental maps of the teaching profession is connected with 'ability' or 'intelligence' or 'potential' – some pupils, it is said, are brighter, cleverer, more able than others, they have more potential. A second is the one alluded to above in the quotation from an article by a union leader and is to do with attitude and behaviour – apathetic/keen, disruptive/co-operative, trouble-making/compliant, and so on. There is a fuller quotation from the article in Box 26.

Box 26

What some teachers expect

This morning many teachers will go to school dreading the prospect of facing a particular class. It could be a class with which last week's lesson went particularly badly, a class where almost every lesson goes badly, or a group with one individual who cannot keep still or keep quiet for more than a few minutes at a time ... Misbehaviour in one lesson can often lead to difficulties for the teacher who takes the children next ...

Unless you have experienced it, it is difficult to imagine the feeling of walking into a classroom in which you know you have to spend the next hour, on your own, trying to create the conditions in which 30 children can learn Shakespeare or simultaneous equations against a background of disruption by children who do not want to learn and do not value the qualification at the end of the road you are travelling together.

John Dunford, general secretary of the Secondary Heads Association, The Guardian, 12 February 2001.

These two continua – 'intelligence' and 'behaviour' – are generally thought of as being independent of each other. So the four corners or quarters of the map can be shown as in the diagram below.

Figure 2: The four corners in teachers' mental maps

B	A
High ability and negative attitude	High ability and positive attitude
D	C
Low ability and negative attitude	Low ability and positive attitude

The 'ideal pupil' (known by researchers as the IP) is in Quadrant A. A class consisting of Quadrant C pupils is easy to teach, but unrewarding. A class of Quadrant D pupils is the kind the union leader was referring to, in teachers' minds the class from hell. But Quadrant B pupils are perhaps the most feared of all – not only challenging and disrespectful but also intelligent and insightful!

Research

Research findings show that pupils perceived by teachers to belong to Quadrant A have much higher achievements than those who are perceived to be in Quadrant D. This is not at all surprising and is precisely what common sense would predict. According to common sense, teachers' expectations are formed on the basis of, and as a result of, pupils' attainments. Research, however, shows that expectations of a particular pupil are often not rooted in objective evidence about that individual but instead in deep seated beliefs and assumptions, many of them tacit or unconscious rather than articulated, to do with social class, gender, ethnicity, culture and race.

For example, pupils' names may affect what is expected even before a teacher has set eyes on them. In Roman times this phenomenon was known as *nomen omen* – knowing someone's name, you have been warned by that alone. When the pupil is met face to face, the teacher may attend in the first instance to entirely non-verbal cues – body-language, gesture, facial expression, demeanour and posture, complexion, physique, use of eye-contact, gait and movement, use of physical space, hairstyle and how tidy it is, how the school uniform is worn, and so on. And then as soon as the pupil opens their mouth, the teacher may be influenced by accent, intonation, use of standard or non-standard terms and syntax, tone, loudness or softness, readiness to interrupt or be interrupted, and appropriacy and register of language when speaking to an authority figure.

All these features are connected with class, gender, culture or sub-culture, ethnicity and race. When a teacher interacts with a pupil, the more similar the pupil is to the teacher in these ways the more likely it is that the teacher will see the pupil as belonging to Quadrant A. The less similar, the more likely that the pupil will be located in Quadrant D.

Box 27

Expectations and inclusion

When adults recall and discuss their own memories of being included or excluded when they were at school, they mention feelings and perceptions such as those summarised here.

Aspects	Perceptions and experiences when I felt included	Perceptions and experiences when I did not feel included
Being known	There's at least one teacher who understands me, knows the real me.	There's this teacher who hasn't a clue what goes on inside me.
Being liked	There's at least one teacher who likes me, is pleased to see me, pleased that I'm in the classroom.	There's this teacher who thinks I'm a waste of space, doesn't want me in their classroom
Questions	I am not afraid to ask questions. The teacher actually encourages me to ask questions, and I enjoy learning through questioning.	I get my head bitten off if I ask questions. The teacher thinks that I think that it's their fault if I haven't understood something. So they assume I'm a trouble-maker.
Praise	I get praised and I feel glad to be in the classroom	I get told off or the teacher's sarcastic and I feel pissed off.
Work	I find the work interesting and enjoyable. It stretches me, and I wouldn't enjoy it so much if it didn't.	The work is boring. Either it's trivial, just set to keep me quiet, or else I can't do it.
Sense of progress	I feel that I'm getting somewhere, the future is bright.	I'm going nowhere, I can't see any future in this.
Adults and institutions	Adults can basically be trusted, and institutions (school, but also for example the police and other authorities) are basically fair.	You can't trust adults and you can't expect to be treated fairly by them, particularly those who have power, for example those who wear a uniform
Reference groups	I care a lot about what the teachers think of me, and about how adults generally see me.	I'm much more concerned about how my friends and mates see me than how authority figures see me. If this gets me into trouble, too bad.

Research shows that pupils perceived by their teachers to be in Quadrant A receive a substantially different educational experience from pupils seen to be in Quadrant D. The differences include:

A climate of respect. Quadrant A pupils feel that they are respected and liked by their teachers. But Quadrant D pupils feel that they are unvalued. Communication of respect and liking, or of lack of recognition and respect, takes place through a range of non-verbal means, not only explicitly.

Feedback. Quadrant A pupils receive more frequent feedback on how they are progressing, and this feedback is not only more positive but also more focused and detailed.

Stimulus. Quadrant A pupils are given more engaging and interesting tasks, and receive more attention related to their learning than their behaviour.

Expression. Quadrant A pupils have more opportunities to ask questions and to clarify their thinking through talk and discussion. If Quadrant D pupils ask questions, it is assumed that they're challenging, confrontational and troublesome. (This point was beautifully echoed in Dickens's observation, quoted in Box 25, of Pip's sister complaining about his tendency to ask questions.)

Justice and trust. Quadrant A pupils feel that the education system, and the world generally, is just and can be trusted. Quadrant D pupils, however, do not easily trust their teachers or their school or authority in the wider world. One consequence is that Quadrant D pupils are much more likely to look for moral support from their peers and from youth culture than from teachers, parents and adults generally.

These abstract points can be brought alive by an inservice training activity such the following. First, the map with its four quadrants is introduced and explained, and participants are asked to sketch their own version. They are then asked to jot memories in each quadrant of times when they were at school or college and were themselves perceived and treated wrongly and unhelpfully. Next, they share these memories in pairs or threes. Then in perhaps slightly larger groupings they note the general differences between Quadrant A and Quadrant D. Finally, they compare and contrast their list with the five points listed above, and with the tabulation in Box 27, 'Expectations and inclusion'.

Multiple intelligences and effective learning

The first and most obvious implication of the discussion above of mental maps is that teachers should strive to see *all* pupils as having the characteristics of Quadrant A pupils, and aim to teach them accordingly. Robert Tauber, an American specialist, says: "Even if a teacher does not truly feel that a particular student is capable of greater achievement or significantly improved behaviour, that teacher can at least *act* as if he or she

---

Box 28

Alternative views of intelligence

Basic questions	Traditional answers	Alternative answers
Is intelligence of a single kind?	Yes. Academics refer to 'G' – general intelligence which is much the same in all fields and subjects.	No. Academics refer to 'multiple intelligences' – at least eight different kinds of intelligence, largely independent of each other.
Is intelligence innate?	Yes. Each person is born with a fixed level of intelligence	No. Intelligence is affected by genetic inheritance but essentially is developed, not innate.
Can intelligence be reliably measured?	Yes.	Perhaps.
If so, how?	A range of paper and pencil tests.	Activities, not pencil and paper.
Can culture-free tests be designed and administered?	Yes.	Almost certainly no.
Can reliable and therefore fair predictions be made, on the basis of tests, about future achievement?	Yes.	No.
Which academic disciplines are most relevant?	Cognitive psychology.	Various, including sociology, social psychology, philosophy and political theory

holds such heightened positive expectations. Who knows, the teacher very well may be convincing to the student and, later, to himself or herself." Such acting (Tauber's highly appropriate word) requires rigorous self-criticism and self-examination, particularly with regard to biases relating to class, race, culture and gender. Otherwise there will be only hypocrisy and tokenism.

Further, and even more valuably and idealistically, teachers can try to scrap the map altogether – discard all or most traditional notions of intelligence and ability, and revise their understandings of disaffection and acceptable behaviour. If indeed they try to operate with a completely new kind of map, one obvious starting place is the work of Howard Gardner on multiple intelligences. Box 28 briefly summarises ways in which his theories differ from traditional theories.

Learning styles

Criticisms and revisions of traditional views of intelligence, as summarised in Box 28, are often accompanied with an emphasis on differences of learning style. A pupil perceived by teachers to have low intelligence or ability, it is argued, probably has a learning style that the education system fails to recognise and appeal to. The theory is initially attractive, for it directs attention to what teachers do and do not do, and away from assumed deficits in pupils. It certainly appears the case that when learning something new both adults and children differ in relation to matters such as the following.

- tolerance of ambiguity and uncertainty, or else desire for clarity and precision
- preparedness or otherwise to make mistakes
- whether they prefer to learn about the whole (the big picture) before the parts, or the parts before the whole

- how much they like visual material, or else prefer text
- how much they like to be active, using their hands and moving around, or prefer to be passively listening and absorbing
- the extent to which they like their emotions to be involved as well as their intellect
- the extent to which they like to consider the human and political implications of the topic under consideration
- the extent to which they are inclined to question and challenge what they are told and the person who is telling them
- whether they enjoy working with symbols and metaphors or whether they prefer to take things literally
- the extent to which they need to talk before they can understand something, or to talk even before they know what their existing ideas are.

Learning style theory acknowledges the existence of such differences and has the following implications, amongst others.

- In every school there is a wide variety of learning preferences amongst the pupils in any class – but all too often classrooms are run as if all the pupils learn in the same way
- Teachers tend to assume, unless they are careful to avoid this, that everyone learns in the same way as they do themselves
- If a pupil has failed to learn something, 'more of the same' teaching may only make things worse, by leading to further demotivation and lower self-confidence
- Other things being equal, everyone benefits from being enabled to extend and develop their learning style or learning repertoire – this often means it is valuable for pupils to reflect on, and be conscious about, their own preferred ways of learning.

The combination of multiple intelligence theory with learning style theory has led in recent years to a body of practice known as 'mind-friendly teaching', or else as 'accelerated learning' or 'effective learning'. In Oakwell this has been summarised as follows:

> The brain develops and functions best in learning environments that stimulate the senses and create

connections between the two hemispheres of the brain; which are high challenge but low stress; where attention is paid to the physical and emotional state of the learner; which view intelligence as modifiable; ... and which provide music, water and fun!

The practical benefits of mind-friendly teaching and accelerated learning include:

- Pupils display increased independence, responsibility and self-direction over the course of the year
- There is significant improvement in the behaviour of pupils previously identified as having behavioural problems
- Co-operative skills improve in all pupils
- The more kinaesthetic pupils benefit from processes of moving frequently from one centre of activity to another

---

There is nothing to smile about

What's wrong with you, miss? Why are you always smiling?' the students at my black-majority school ask me. 'I smile because I see you,' is my habitual reply.

But what I want to say is something like this: 'I smile to salute you, to salute all the learners here, who continue to hold tight to their dignity and self-belief in the endless and ugly face of racism, rejection and poverty. I smile to salute our teachers who work more hours than there are, before and after school, in holidays and at weekends, to struggle beside our students to try, through mentoring, after-school classes, residential courses, to restore the balance and open the doors in a closed and unbalanced world.'

That's what I hope they hear in my smile. But even that ignores the poignancy of their question, their subtext that says a smile – respect, recognition, affirmation – is so unexpected as to be a symptom of illness, of deviance, their message that announces that there is nothing to smile about.

Quoted in *The Future of Multi-Ethnic Britain*, Profile Books, 2000

Box 29

Accelerated learning – some teachers' views

Scientific research

How do you ensure a calm and orderly learning environment? How do you use a variety of teaching strategies to motivate pupils? How do you meet the differing learning needs of all the pupils in your class? How do you get pupils to retain information long enough to pass exams? Along with so many other teachers, these are the kind of endless yet essential questions which I had long grappled with but had never achieved really comprehensive answers to. That was until I attended a course in Oakwell on accelerated learning. As the day progressed I realised that, almost unbelievably, I was being presented with a framework which seemed to answer all my questions. Perhaps even more impressive, it was a framework based not on value judgements but on scientific research on how the brain works and was accompanied by a myriad of practical strategies to use in the classroom.

Our brains were refreshed

The two and a half day of inset for the senior management team had all the vital ingredients of a really good course: information was presented in a multitude of ways; there were highly challenging activities; others were highly challenging activities and opportunities for individual and group reflection; there was lots of laughter and lots of excellent sandwiches. Our brains refreshed and filled with the theories of Visual-Auditory-Kinaesthetic and multiple intelligences, we sat down on the last afternoon to plan an intensive two-day introduction to accelerated learning for the 60+ teaching staff in the school the following month.

He could now understand

... I informed parents what the topic would be at our Annual Parents Meeting. I gave them a thumbnail sketch about accelerated learning and the eight intelligences and told them if they wanted to know more about what kind of learners their children were, then they would find out more at the meeting on 17 February at 7pm. We always have a staff sweepstake on how many parents will turn up the annual meeting. It's usually something between 12 and 24, though one year it was 30. On this occasion I won the sweepstake with an estimate of 40. Actually, 56 parents turned up and the room was packed to capacity ... One parent, a young father of two children, shook my hand and thanked me three times because he could now understand why his two young children were so different in their learning habits.

Source: newsletter issued in Oakwell

- Leadership skills emerge in most pupils. Pupils who have not previously displayed leadership abilities take the lead with their group, particularly in music and art, and in collaborative group work
- Parents report that behaviour improves at home and that children show more positive attitudes to school
- Daily work with music and movement helps pupils retain information. At the end of the year, for example, pupils may remember academic information which they learnt through songs as early as the previous September
- The role of the teacher changes as the year progresses, becoming less directive and more facilitative, more diversified, less that of a taskmaster and more that of a resource person and guide
- Pupils become progressively more skilled at working effectively in this unique and non-traditional classroom format.

In common with certain other authorities, Oakwell has given a high profile to accelerated learning in recent years. The responses and reactions of Oakwell teachers are shown in Box 29.

MESSAGES FROM A CONSULTANCY

I like PSHE when we have debates and all that. It's boring when you're not allowed to talk and have debates; when it's just working, writing, copying from the board.

Sometimes the teachers see you're trying hard to stay calm and work, and they back off a bit. But then other teachers, they really push you to the limit.

One thing that really gets on my nerves is when we get into trouble and it's not our fault. The other day, me and my friends, we got into trouble, but some white pupils were behaving worse that us and they didn't get into trouble.

When you put your hand up, they never ask you the question. They only ask you when you obviously don't know the answer.

You've got to respect your elders, yeah, but it just makes me so angry. Why do we have to respect them if they keep putting us down.

I like Miss ----, because she knows we're different. We're not all the same and so I can have a chat with her.

In my last school I used to tell the headteacher there was a girl who was being racist, and stopping me playing netball. She said she'd sort it out, but she didn't really care.

Teachers don't want to talk about racism in school, because it's sensitive.

Extracts from a focus group discussion, Oakwell secondary school

Learning styles and race equality

It is sometimes claimed that each person's learning style is as distinctive as their fingerprint. This is a valuable metaphor if it directs attention to each pupil as an individual, and encourages teachers not to 'treat all children the same'. It is a wrong and dangerous generalisation, however, if it implies that learning style is unrelated to the immediate subject-matter being studied; to the pattern of relationships in a classroom between teacher and pupils and between pupils; to issues of institutional and cultural racism; and to a pupil's sense of personal, cultural and ethnic identity.

The vast majority of discourse about accelerated learning, multiple intelligences and learning styles is colour-blind and culture-blind – it fails to take into account concepts and experiences of ethnic and cultural diversity, and fails to recognise that schools and classrooms, and the teachers and learners within them, are affected by colour and cultural racism.

Time and again, when new ideas are implemented in colour-blind ways, black people are disadvantaged. For this reason alone it is important that theories of multiple intelligences and diverse learning styles should be examined critically. There are other reasons too, however. For the theories do appear, at first sight, to be highly relevant to issues of race equality and cultural diversity in education. If used critically and appropriately – i.e. *not* in colour-blind ways – they appear to have great potential for raising attainment of Asian, black and other 'minority' pupils. There are four implications of this for staff training, and for the further development of theory.

First, when teachers become more interested in and sensitive to differences of learning style amongst their pupils, they may also become more interested and sensitive in relation to differences of culture, language, narrative and community; to differing senses of personal and cultural identity and Britishness; and to differing experiences of racism. But these latter kinds of sensitivity do not follow inevitably from an interest in diverse learning styles and modes of intelligence. They must be explicitly focused on.

Second, theories of accelerated learning valuably place emphasis on the creation of secure learning environments – places where all pupils feel safe and

affirmed. All should be enabled to feel 'IALACAS': 'I am Likeable and Capable and Significant'. The B-A-S-I-S of a good classroom is to do with Belonging, Aspirations, Safety, Identity and Success. So far so good. But 'belonging' has to be conceptualised with awareness that not all British people are permitted or encouraged to feel that they belong to the nation (see Chapter 5 for further discussion of this); aspirations can be limited by discrimination on grounds of race, religion or culture; safety can be threatened by racist behaviour and language on the streets and in the school playground (Chapter 6); identity is embedded in a range of different communities, and within each person's sense of identity there are often tensions and conflicts; success in society at large is rarer for certain communities than for others, because of patterns of inequality and unfairness. All these points must be borne in mind. They are discussed at greater length elsewhere in this book – see in particular Chapter 5 on identities, and the material in Chapters 2 and 6 on racism.

> Box 30
>
> ## Not one point on a compass
>
> I never learnt one thing about black British history or culture at school. It was entirely possible to go through school in Stevenage and not know that black people existed at all (other than the few you saw on television or around the town) let alone that they had been in Britain for centuries. Nobody told me that there were at least two black women in the Scottish royal court in 1513; that Olaudah Equiano, an Igbo from eastern Nigeria, toured the country during the latter part of the eighteenth century putting the case for the abolition of the slave trade. No one mentioned that the country's first race riot took place in Butetown near Cardiff in 1919, or that the first black MP, Shapurji Saklatvala, a Parsee, was elected to represent North Battersea in 1922. There was not one word that would have located me in the country in which I was born, not one scrap of information to challenge those among my peers who knew no better than to repeat their parents' claims that I had just come off the banana boat and was now (I never did get this) set both to steal their jobs and sponge off the welfare state. Nothing. Not one point on a compass that would have helped me navigate my way from my mother's past to my own present.
>
> This chasm in my education was thanks largely to the collective and selective myopia that Britain has about its place in world history, but at the coal face that was my school the crime was negligence rather than anything sinister. It is not as though my teachers deliberately went out to deny me access to my own history. My guess would be that most of them didn't know any of this themselves.
>
> Gary Younge, *No Place Like Home*, 2000.

Third, learning style theory has the potential to help teachers have high expectations of a wider range of pupils than if they operate with traditional views of intelligence (see Box 28). Also, it can provide valuable reminders that disruption and disaffection amongst pupils can be caused or reinforced by inappropriate and insensitive styles of teaching. But learning style theory does not inherently require teachers to review their own biases and expectations relating to issues of class, gender, ethnicity and culture; it does not necessarily require them to learn and use skills of cross-cultural literacy; it does not inevitably enforce recognition that certain pupils, their families and communities are targets of overt racism. There is still a need, therefore, to consider such issues explicitly if learning style theory is to be as valuable as it could be.

Fourth, if teachers do eschew colour-blind approaches there are grave dangers of stereotyping – 'minority pupils tend to have kinaesthetic learning styles', for example. It may indeed be the case, however, that the culture of some communities is connected with, and reinforces, certain learning styles. Some cultures put high emphasis on co-operation and collaboration, for example, and are suspicious of competition as a

motivating factor in learning. Some place high value on indirect expression, for example story-telling, metaphor and symbol, and on oracy and articulacy as distinct from writing. Some like to use visual and pictorial expression as well as texts and prefer engagement, interaction and challenge rather than passive and docile listening. Teachers need to be sensitive to such cultural differences, and indeed this is one of the senses in which they should not be colour-blind or culture-blind. But they must at the same time guard against the dangers of stereotyping and of failing to recognise the distinctive needs of any one pupil at a particular time.

Forming and nourishing great expectations is a collective matter for teachers, not just a matter for individuals. This is particularly important when not only conceptions of intelligence and disaffection have to be addressed but also matters of ethnicity, class and culture. There needs to be much discussion in every staffroom and every staff team – not least because it is in staffroom culture that damaging mental maps may be perpetuated and reinforced unless they are explicitly challenged. Further, the organisational structures of each school must be kept under review, to check that they really do signal high expectations. Paramount amongst these are processes of selection, setting and streaming.

On occasions of great catastrophe, for example a major train crash or an earthquake, medical staff engage in a system of triage – the injured are divided into three categories. Those whose injuries are slight do not receive immediate treatment, nor do those whose situation is hopeless. Resources are devoted in the first instance to 'suitable cases for treatment'. A number of researchers and commentators have suggested that this is an accurate metaphor for British education, particularly since the advent of league tables – resources are allegedly allocated according to a triage system. Certain pupils – those in Quadrant A (see Figure 1) – are expected to do well enough so far as league tables are concerned and significant resources are therefore not allocated to them. Pupils in Quadrant D are seen as no-hopers, so precious resources are not wasted on them. Pupils in the other two quadrants are seen as suitable cases for treatment – potentially able to improve their school's place in league tables if special attention is paid to them. Within this overall picture, African-Caribbean and Pakistani pupils are disproportionately perceived by the education system to be in Quadrant D, and therefore unworthy of precious resources. Tackling the triage system in British education involves much more than sensitivity to different learning styles, crucially important though such sensitivity is.

Visibility and recognition

It is essential, to summarise, to complement learning style theory with antiracism. The theory will not be adequate to generate successful practice if it is colour-blind or culture-blind. Schools and teachers must not blinker themselves from the realities of colour and cultural racism and of street and institutional racism. In his book *Invisible Man*, the African-American writer Ralph Ellison famously used imagery of seeing and not-seeing to describe the mental map with which white people view black people. He said:

> When they [white people] approach me they see only my surroundings, themselves, or figments of their imagination – indeed everything and anything except me ... That invisibility to which I refer occurs because of a peculiar disposition of the eyes of those with whom I come in contact. A matter of the construction of their inner eyes, those eyes with which they look through their physical eyes upon reality.

The distinction between physical eyes and inner eyes can be applied to teaching and education. If white teachers are to have higher expectations of black children and young people, they have to examine – and be prepared to change – their inner eyes.

Ellison's metaphors about seeing recall Charles Taylor's concept of recognition, quoted in the previous chapter. A person's identity, Taylor writes, is 'shaped by recognition or its absence, often by the misrecognition of others'. His point has profound implications for school classrooms. 'Nonrecognition or misrecognition can inflict harm, can be a form of oppression, imprisoning someone in a false, distorted and reduced mode of being.' The dangers are well illustrated in Gary Younge's autobiographical reflections on his education in Stevenage, quoted in Box 30. Only if pupils' stories and identities are recognised, Younge stresses, can they develop a compass for understanding themselves and the world, and their place in the stories of their society. There is a further quotation from Younge's memories at the start of Chapter 6, and this too is about the essential importance of young people's stories and experiences being recognised and taken seriously. His points in Box 30 about personal identity and national narrative are explored further in the next chapter, entitled 'We all have a story to tell'.

5 We all have a story to tell
– identity, community and society

Going to leave the world gobsmacked

'We are slowly becoming the best country', writes a 12-year-old pupil. 'I'm looking forward to the future, what potential we have. A new generation of children ... so many windows to learning different cultures and languages ...One day in twenty years time we're going to achieve something that is going to leave the world gobsmacked ... I look in the mirror, who do I see? A president, lawyer, politician ...' The full text is in Box 31.

The pupil quoted in Box 31 writes as a young black South African. His feelings about his country and its collective future, and about himself and his personal future, are of relevance everywhere. Do children in Britain develop a similar confidence in their society's future and in their own capacity to help shape it? How do they picture Britain and how do they understand Britain's story and stories? How do their own stories and the stories of their family and neighbourhood intertwine with larger and grander narratives about the nation? What are the implications for the teaching of history and current affairs, and for programmes of personal and social education and citizenship education? These are the questions addressed in this chapter. There are four headings:

- Here and now
- This country
- Community of communities
- Difference and disagreement

Here and now

As part of the Inclusive Classrooms, Inclusive Schools project, a primary school in Oakwell organised a major project entitled 'We are Norstead Now' – Norstead being a well-known area of the borough whose population has long been culturally diverse. The core of the project was the creation of a three-dimensional work of art about the communities who live in Norstead, opened formally by the borough's mayor. Parents and other adult members of local communities were involved from the start. As part of the project, children wrote about their experiences of living in Britain and their poems and prose were displayed at the school and also at Oakwell education offices and the professional development centre. One of the poems succinctly summarised the themes of the project as a whole:

I Love My Country

What a long way we have come from apartheid to here. We are slowly becoming the best country and no matter how much anybody moans, we have the third most recognised flag in the world. Fifty three percent of the world's gold comes from South Africa.

What a mess we were in but that doesn't matter, I'm looking forward to thefuture, soon our country's going to be so high tech we shall be able to have flying cars, well maybe I'm over exaggerating but what potential we have. The crime rates are going down and we might even become the safest country in the world.

A new future with life, a new generation of children who do not take people by their creed or colour. I love South African football, what potential we have there, and of course the rainbow nation, so many windows to learning different cultures and languages, eleven to be exact, English, Afrikaans, Zulu, Xhosa, Sipedi, Venda, Ndebele, Tswana, Sotho, Siswati, Xitonga.

I look in the mirror, who do I see? A president, lawyer, politician or maybe even a doctor. Time will tell. And one day South Africa is going to achieve something in twenty years time that is going to leave the world gobsmacked.

Peace, affection and most of all love.

Buhle (aged 12), summer 2002

We all have a story to tell

Many different faces.
Many different cultures we live within.
We may be different but we are all one.
We all have a past.
We all have a story to tell.
Many people are here because of war and suffering,
But whatever the reason
We unite together.

As well as summarising the themes of the project, the poem also summarises the themes of this chapter and, more generally, major aspects of citizenship education in Britain in coming decades. There is a stress on difference and diversity, both of race and of culture, but also on similarity and equality, and shared commitments and responsibilities in one place. There are differences in personal and community experience, but everyone's story is of equal value. The young writer has a sense of the school's pupils coming from a range of different countries, cultures and experiences, but going forward together to make Norstead in particular, and by extension the whole of Britain, a better place. The poem illustrates well the importance of starting in the here and now before turning towards abstract concepts of equality, cultural diversity and social cohesion, and before studying British and world history in ways that give pupils a sense of all belonging to the same overall narrative.

The transition from the here and now of Norstead to concepts of world community sounds, and indeed is, enormous. The children nevertheless felt comfortable with it, judging by their writing. One girl, for example, wrote this:

Difference and sharing

We come to this country to see different people,
To learn different languages and to feel safe.
Some people are poor. Some people are rich.
They will meet together and start to be friends.
It's not a big problem what colour you are.
We come here to feel safe.
We should know what is happening in other countries.
The earth spins around and people grow up.
People change countries and attitudes.
We know our world is big enough for everyone.
So we should all share it.

The poems were upbeat, hopeful and idealistic but did not deny the realities of racism, prejudice and hurt in the here and now. One boy, for example, wrote:

Sad eyes

My friend has sad eyes,
Someone teased him about his race.
I said to that person,
'It doesn't matter what race you are,
It doesn't matter what religion you are.'

We all live in the same country,
And we should learn about each other,
Also think about other people's feelings.

Box 32

Curiosity and self-esteem

* Children's speaking and learning skills improved

* They developed confidence in participating in group discussions

* They became more aware of the range of cultures in our school

* Their motivation and enthusiasm inspired them to produce excellent written work

* Their behaviour and attitudes improved

* They developed a sense of curiosity and interest in other children's cultural backgrounds

* Their self-esteem rose

* Parents were extremely appreciative and began coming into the school more often and interacting with staff with greater confidence

* It was a rewarding experience for all concerned

Conclusions in the report on We Are Norstead Now

The world is for everyone to share,
And not just for one person.
So share and be happy.

After the project was over, the staff responsible for it wrote a brief evaluation. There is a summary in Box 32. The children were also asked to write evaluations. What did they understand to be the project's aims? What did they consider they were learning? One girl wrote:

We are doing this project because we all want to know about different countries. It means a lot to me because I feel very special and important. My mum is very happy for me because I have the chance to share stories about my country. I came to this country because it was very hard for my parents to get a job in Latvia. So it was difficult because they didn't have enough money. My mum is Jewish and my dad is Russian.

And a boy wrote:

We are doing this project because we are representing our country. It means a lot to me because I'm representing my own country, Iraq. I've learnt about other cultures and that there are so many different types of people that come from other countries. I came here because in my country there was a lot of fighting and we didn't have enough money or food. This country, London, means a lot to me because I grew up here and I'm more used to English things. I left Iraq when I was one year old but I would like to go back once there is peace.

Easy

The United Kingdom of Great Britain and Northern Ireland,
That's a long name for home.
Somalia's easier.
Southall's easy too.

Quoted in *In Exile: the magazine of refugee rights*, July 2002

This country

The boy quoted above refers to 'this country, London' and contrasts it 'with my own country, Iraq'. It is unlikely that he believes that London is the name of a country – even if he does, he is aware that the adjective associated with it is 'English'. His error is a significant slip of the pen, however, since many people identify with a city or town more readily than with a country. Most of the people in an area such as Norstead, with its strong sense of local identity, see is as part of a city, not as part of a local authority – their larger identity is Londoner, not Oakwellian. Further, the notion of 'this country' is not at all as clear as is conventionally assumed. When the academic journal *Political Quarterly* produced a special issue on national identity in 2000 to welcome the millennium, its editors wryly remarked:

The British have long been distinguished by having no clear idea about who they are, where they are, or what they are. Most of them have routinely described England as Britain. Only businesspeople talk about a place called the United Kingdom. It is all a terrible muddle.

It is important that children throughout Britain should be helped to make sense of the muddle that history has bequeathed to them. Muddle can be confusing and

dispiriting – but also can be consoling and exhilarating. Children need to understand that Britishness is not something fixed and final but has always been contested; that it has evolved and changed over the centuries; and that it is evolving still. They will then more readily grasp that there are many ways of being British, and that taking pride in one's Britishness (or Englishness or whatever) is not intrinsically exclusionary, racist or xenophobic. They will enjoy the challenges that diversity presents and see that they themselves have a part and a stake in Britain's unfolding future. Such feelings and intentions were well expressed in the poems quoted above – 'we should know what is happening in other countries', 'this world is for everyone to share', 'we all unite together'.

Disentangling the 'terrible muddle' involves consideration of constitutional history. It was only after the Union with Scotland (1707) that England, Scotland and Wales became known as Great Britain. From 1801 to 1922 Ireland was joined to Great Britain and the state's name changed to the United Kingdom. After Partition (1922) the state's name changed again, becoming what it is now, the United Kingdom of Great

We Are Britain

This book takes a poetic look at thirteen young British people as they work, rest and play. None of these children want to live in a world where everybody looks like them; they are all ready to embrace a multicultural, multicoloured land where every child is equal and all children have a poem to call their own. If Britain is going to be great in the future, it will be because these kids want curry and chips, mangoes and strawberries and banana crumble, and they think of all of these as British.

The British are not a single tribe, or a single religion, and we don't come from a single place. But we are building a home where we are all able to be who we want to be, yet still be British.

That is what we do: we take, we adapt, and we move forward.

We are the British. We are Britain!

From the introduction to *We Are Britain* by Benjamin Zephaniah, 2002

Britain and Northern Ireland. But these bald historical facts do not correspond to how terms are actually used. Many people use the terms 'United Kingdom', 'Great Britain' and 'Britain' interchangeably, as if all three terms refer to precisely the same place and always have done. In England, there is confusion in everyday conversation about whether other parts of the UK are 'countries', 'nations' or 'provinces'. Such semantic questions are not without relevance in this book, but it would not be appropriate to go into them in detail. There is substantial scholarly discussion of them, rooted in a magisterial survey of history over many centuries, in *The Isles* by Norman Davies (Macmillan, 1999) and a shorter discussion, focusing more on the present and recent past, in Jeremy Paxman's *The English* (Penguin, 1999).

In addition to semantic and constitutional matters, there are issues to do with how the history of Britain is summarised and with how British society is pictured in the present. A summary of key historical points appears in Box 33, taken from the introduction to Simon Schama's *A History of Britain*, published in connection with his series on BBC television. Schama was keen to tell the story of Britain as 'a grand narrative', but also to challenge those dominant interpretations of history that portray unchanging and longstanding traditions rather than constant re-negotiation and change.

Scholars sometimes distinguish between 'hegemonic narratives' on the one hand and 'counter narratives' on the other. With regard to stories about Britain, the distinction is illustrated in Box 34. At an inservice training course the material in Box 34 can be presented in the first instance as a cloze exercise – some of the details are left blank, and participants are asked to guess what the missing points are, working in twos or threes. Such an activity makes an appropriate introduction to the material in Box 35, about Britain as an imagined community.

Britain as an imagined community

The concept of 'imagined community' was central in the discussion of national identity in *The Future of Multi-Ethnic Britain*. To call Britain a community is to speak metaphorically. Its members are not literally bound together in tight-knit, face-to-face relationships, as in a village. Most citizens are strangers to one another, for each has met only a minute proportion of fellow citizens.

Box 33

A history of Britain

Imagine a British history in which alteration, mutation and flux, rather than continuity and bedrock solidity, is the norm; a history that does not lead inexorably to a consummation in the unitary state of Great Britain but that sees that period – only, after all, three centuries old, barely as long as Roman Britannia – as just one epoch among many in the evolution of our island nations.

This would be a history in which national identity – not just in Britain, or in England, but in Scotland, Ireland and Wales – was not a fixed but a decidedly shifting and fluid quality; a history in which the allegiance that mattered might, from generation to generation, from place to place, be a matter of clan or class, town or manor, language or dialect, church or club, guild or family, rather than of flag and dynasty.

It would be a history in which the ragged frontiers of regions might count for a lot more than the fixed borders of countries; in which north-south divisions within Scotland and Wales could be as profound as those between either of them and their English neighbour.

It would be an elastic history of nationhood with England or Scotland sometimes closer in spirit and interest to France or even to Rome than to each other; but at other times genuinely and wholeheartedly (for good or ill) bound together within the British union...

Simon Schama, *A History of Britain*, BBC Publications, 2000

Also, few people have visited more than a small proportion of their country's cities and conurbations, let alone its towns and villages. Nevertheless, large numbers of people share an idea of the nation and what it stands for, and feel that they have important things in common with millions of others. Box 35 shows how various writers have imagined Britain over the last 50 years or so. It can be used to stimulate discussion at an inservice course for teachers, and as the basis for an exercise to

Box 34

Points and stories about Britain over the years

Aspects	Dominant points and stories	Alternative points and stories
Age	Britain is very old – at least 1,000 years.	In its present form, Britain has existed only since 1922. It did not exist at all until 1707.
Geography	'This sceptr'd isle ... this England' (John of Gaunt, in *Richard II* by William Shakespeare)	England is not an island. In both John of Gaunt's time and in Shakespeare's there were two 'sceptres' in the island of Britain, not one.
Unity	Britain has always been a harmonious, unified and united place.	The history of the British Isles is a story of continuous argument and disagreement, and frequently of armed conflict.
Change	Over the centuries there has been very little change or dislocation.	The story of Britain is a story of continual change.
Democracy	There is a long tradition of democracy.	It was only in the twentieth century that women and people over 18 were allowed to vote. Most aspects of modern democracy were bitterly resisted by Britain's rulers when they were first proposed.
Independence	Essentially, Britain is isolated from all other countries, and its history can and should be studied independently from that of other countries.	In all important aspects of life – culture, law, politics, science, economics, religion – Britain has always been connected to the wider world.
Monarchy	The kings and queens of England, and since 1707 those of Britain, have symbolised Englishness and Britishness.	Many monarchs and their spouses have spoken English as an additional language, if at all. Since 1707 no British-born woman has married the king or the heir to the throne, apart from Princess Diana.

explore the concept of imagined community further. A broadly similar exercise can be used with pupils.

The quotations in Box 35 show that an imagined community has a range of different components, including the following:

The sense and sensations of home – the recurring sights, sounds, smells and tastes that 'bring it all back to me', and make someone feel 'at home where I belong'.

Custom and ceremony – events and actions that are performed regularly, for example weekly or annually, perhaps even every day, that give the individual a sense of identity and continuity and at the same time link individuals to larger groups and patterns.

Public spaces – institutions such as schools, hospitals, the legal system and the transport system, and areas such as shops, streets, parks and places of entertainment and recreation, where people mingle with people they do not know personally.

Story and narrative – the key events, developments and achievements in national history, and major talking points in current and recent news, and perhaps also in soap operas on radio and TV.

Box 35

Britain as an imagined community

The England I want to come home to

For me, England stands for the Church of England, eccentric incumbents, oil-lit churches, Women's Institutes, modest village inns, arguments about cow-parsley on the altar, the noise of mowing machines on Saturday afternoons, local newspapers, local auctions, the poetry of Tennyson, Crabbe, Hardy and Matthew Arnold, local talent, local concerts, a visit to the cinema, branch-line trains, light railways, leaning on gates and looking across fields ... I know the England I want to come home to is not very different from that in which you want to live. If it were some efficient ant-heap which the glass and steel, flat-roof, straight-roof boys want to make it, then how could we love it as we do?

John Betjeman, broadcast talk, 1943

What I loved about Britain

Suddenly, in the space of a moment, I realised what it was that I loved about Britain – which is to say, all of it. Every last bit of it, good and bad – Marmite, village fetes, country lanes, people saying 'mustn't grumble' and 'I'm terribly sorry but', people apologising to me when I conk them with a careless elbow, milk in bottles, beans on toast, haymaking in June, stinging nettles, seaside piers, Ordnance Survey maps, crumpets, hot-water bottles as a necessity, drizzly Sundays – every bit of it ... What other nation in the world could have given us William Shakespeare, pork pies, Christopher Wren, Windsor Great Park, the Open University, *Gardeners' Question Time*, and the chocolate digestive biscuit? None, of course.

Bill Bryson, *Notes from a Small Island*, 1996

Will still be

Fifty years from now Britain will still be the country of long shadows on county grounds, warm beer, invincible green suburbs, dog lovers and pools fillers and ... old maids cycling to holy communion through the early morning mist.

John Major, 1993

And so on

... 'I know my rights', village cricket and Elgar, Do-It-Yourself, punk, street fashion, irony, vigorous politics, brass bands, Shakespeare, Cumberland sausages, double-decker buses, Vaughan Williams, Donne and Dickens, twitching net curtains, breast obsession, quizzes and crosswords, country churches, dry-stone walls, gardening, Christopher Wren and Monty Python, easy-going Church of England vicars, the Beatles, bad hotels and good beer, church bells, Constable and Piper, finding foreigners funny, David Hare and William Cobbett, drinking to excess, Women's Institutes, fish and chips, curry, Christmas Eve at King's College Cambridge, indifference to food, civility and crude language, fell-running, ugly caravan sites on beautiful cliff tops, crumpets, Bentleys and Reliant Robins, and so on.

Jeremy Paxman, *The English*, 1998

Sights and sounds

The sights and sounds of Britain, for us, include Harold Wilson, and Enoch Powell and Ted Heath, and the shuffling queues in a dole office, and the sound of a Salvation Army band, and the naughty chirruping of the voices over the crackling radio airwaves when we switched on for 'Round the Horne', and the smell of wax on the floor of a public library, and the roar of the crowd at the Arsenal football stadium, and the antiseptic lines of beds in a ward at the old St George's Hospital, and a moonscape of rusted metal in Trafford, and the unexpected perfume of wild flowers in an abandoned railway bed.

Mike and Trevor Phillips, *Windrush: the irresistible rise of multiracial Britain*, 1998

An inservice activity around these four broad categories can have several stages, as follows:

- Participants write down examples under each of the four headings, taken from the details in Box 35.

- They add examples of their own.

- They select ten examples as being particularly significant. The question then is how *inclusive* the examples are. Do they include both women and men? Young and old? All parts of the United Kingdom? All social classes? Both country and town? A wide range in terms of race, ethnicity, religion and cultural heritage? The point is obvious, but nevertheless worth spelling out: most of the examples in the first four quotations in Box 35 are *not* inclusive. On the contrary, they totally omit large sections of the population, or else leave them marginalised and unrecognised.

- As individuals or as groups, they compile their own versions of the lists in Box 35, trying to make the lists as inclusive as possible.

- They discuss and clarify the implications of the exercise for their own school and their own teaching. For example, they devise analogous exercises for their pupils, focusing less on the national sense of imagined community and more on personal and local community (as in 'We Are Norstead Now'), and on the school community itself.

In all discussions of belonging and national identity a key distinction needs to be drawn between affection for one's own country and hostility towards others. The two do not necessarily go together. The distinction is well expressed in the extract in Box 36. Later in the chapter there is fuller discussion of images of 'the other', and of how views of the other can be open, positive and co-operative rather than suspicious and fearful.

Box 36

England, with all thy faults

'England, with all thy faults, I love thee still, My country!' (Cowper) is about right. People everywhere love their own country, just as we love family, home, garden or local landscape. Life without deep affection for the familiar for its own sake is almost unthinkable. But these strong natural sentiments turn into absurd and potentially dangerous nationalism when elevated into a general theory of the superiority of your own kind, your own people, your own language simply because it is yours.

Polly Toynbee, *The Guardian*, 12 January 2000

Community of communities

The value of the exercise outlined above is that it stresses how difficult it is, but also how important it is, to picture Britain as a single community. *The Future of Multi-Ethnic Britain* argued that Britain should be pictured as 'a community of communities', both in the past and in the present, not as a monolithic whole. Its principal points in this regard were as follows:

'Majority'/'minority'

The picture of Britain as a 94/6 society – where ninety-four per cent are imagined to belong to one vast majority since they are white and six per cent to various minorities since they are not – is not an accurate one. For the so-called majority contains vast differences in terms of social class, outlook, lifestyle and experience. There are also significant differences relating to gender, age and region. And it is outrageously untrue to imply that so-called minorities have more in common with each other than they do with people in the majority. Ideally, terms such as 'majority' and 'minority' should not be used. They are particularly inappropriate in London boroughs such as Oakwell, where the term 'minority' is mathematically inaccurate or misleading. The main objections to the term 'minority', however, are that it all too often implies 'less important' or 'marginal' and that it wrongly assumes the existence of a majority within which there are no significant differences and conflicts.

Every community is in a process of development; each has its own internal tensions, arguments and contradictions; each overlaps with several others; each influences and impacts on, and is in turn influenced by, others.

A single system but with arguments and controversy

When the *SS Windrush* docked in 1948 it was not in a foreign country. The journey had been an internal one, from one part of a single system – the British Empire – to another. Similarly Africans, Bangladeshis, Indians, Irish, Pakistanis and many others came from one part of a single system to another. 'We are here because you were there.'

Nor was the country where the SS Windrush docked politically and ideologically united. On the contrary, the ship came to a land riven by debates and disputes which pre-dated its arrival by centuries. Britain was already culturally and ideologically diverse and contained a range of self-understandings and stories. Box 34 contrasts key aspects of the dominant images and stories of Britain that until recently were taught or implied in schools, and that continue to be prevalent and influential in the media.

As with communities so with individuals. No one is purely one thing. It is important to recall that all or most pupils have a range of affiliations and loyalties, and that some of these may be in competition or even conflict. No human being can be reduced to a category and therefore the individuality of any one person is all too easily neglected when large categories are being used – categories such as African, African-Caribbean, Black, British, Chinese, Christian, English, Indian, Irish, Jewish, Kashmiri, Muslim, Panjabi, Sikh, South Asian or Traveller, and so on. People's sense of cultural and personal identity develops over time and is different in different surrounding contexts. At all times and in all contexts, however, some of the components in one's identity are less 'tradeable' than others – less open to negotiation, questioning and change.

Shared space and shared future

People in Britain have many differences. But they inhabit the same space and share the same future. 'Britain' is the name of the space which they all share. Some groups have more weight and power than others, but no group or community owns Britain. It is no one's

sole possession. All have a role in the collective project of fashioning Britain as an outward-looking, generous, inclusive society.

The fundamental need, both practical and theoretical, is to treat people equally and with due regard and respect for difference; and to treasure the rights and freedoms of individuals but also belonging, cohesion and solidarity. Neither equality nor respect for difference is a sufficient value on its own. They must be held together, mutually challenging and supportive, and both must be enriched and qualified by the need for social cohesion.

Difference and disagreement

A community of communities contains conflicts of interests and values – it is not one happy family. Not only in wider society but also in schools and classrooms, ways have to be found for handling disagreements both respectfully and firmly. 'What happens when people disagree?' is the fundamental question of all politics and the essential underlying question in all programmes of citizenship education and personal and social education.

In the paragraphs that follow, the question is approached in three ways. First, there is discussion of 'images of the other', namely images of people with whom one is in conflict. Second, the official objectives of citizenship education in Britain are briefly re-visited and some small but significant additions are proposed. Third, there are notes on handling controversial issues in classroom discussions and informal conversations between staff and pupils.

Images of the other

When the Runnymede Trust Commission on Islamophobia published a consultation paper in 1997 it quoted critically from an article by a prominent journalist. Islam was once, he said, 'a great civilisation worthy of being argued with'. But latterly it had degenerated into 'a primitive enemy fit only to be sensitively subjugated'. Seeing himself quoted in the consultation paper, the journalist published a defiant response. He entitled it 'I believe in Islamophobia' and concluded: 'To worry about contemporary Islam is not mad. It would be mad to do otherwise.' The response of the Commission to his article was to stress that a distinction needs to be made between unfounded ('phobic') hostility to Islam on the one hand and reasoned disagreement or criticism on the other.

The commission argued in this connection that a prior distinction needs to be made between *closed* views of Islam on the one hand and *open* views on the other. Phobic dread of Islam is the recurring characteristic of closed views. Legitimate disagreement and criticism, as also appreciation and respect, are aspects of open views. In summary form, the eight distinctions between closed and open views were to do with:

- whether Islam is seen as monolithic and static, or as diverse and dynamic

- whether Islam is seen as other and separate, or as similar and interdependent

- whether Islam is seen as inferior, or as different but equal

- whether Islam is seen as an aggressive enemy or as a cooperative partner

- whether Muslims are seen as manipulative or as sincere

- whether Muslim criticisms of 'the West' are rejected or debated

- whether discriminatory behaviour against Muslims is defended or opposed

- whether anti-Muslim discourse is seen as natural or as problematic.

Three years later the Commission on the Future of Multi-Ethnic Britain adopted the eight distinctions proposed by the earlier commission, and suggested that they could be applied to all major value conflicts in and between modern societies. Box 37 shows the scheme that was proposed. The box does not refer specifically to hostility towards Islam but to all hostility towards 'the other'.

At an inservice training session the eight categories in Box 37 can be introduced to teachers by requesting them first to consider their own views of Ofsted inspectors. For such an activity the eight categories can be presented as in Box 38. The activity is light-hearted and usually entertaining but it strikingly and valuably explains and illustrates the eight points. Instead of Ofsted, there are many alternative 'others', including LEA officers, parents, governors and pupils. Box 38 can readily be adapted to any of these.

Citizenship education

The discussions so far in this chapter have significant implications for the objectives and key ideas in citizenship education and PSE. Box 40 is derived in its basic structure from the Curriculum 2000 documents issued by the QCA. But several of the items have been slightly adapted to take into account the references in this chapter to personal, local and national identities and its discussion of images of the other.

Controversy in classrooms and conversations

At almost any time, teachers may find themselves having to respond to questions from pupils about matters of opinion on which society is divided. The questions and comments are put indirectly and through behaviour as well as explicitly. By the same token, the answers which adults give are communicated through behaviour, tone and attitude as well as directly. In the *Times Educational Supplement* shortly after 11 September 2001, it was reported that teachers were currently having to address questions such as the following:

- Will there be a war? Will my family be in danger?

- Why did God let this happen?

- Why is Osama bin Laden suddenly a bad person when during the time he fought the Russians he was a good person?

- Why should we believe in religion when bad things happen because of it?

- Why do Arabs hate the Americans?

- Is Osama bin Laden guilty?

- Why should I bother at school if there is going to be a war?

- What will happen to the Afghanistan refugees?

How to reply or respond to such questions and to the concerns and notions behind them? Often replies have to be given on the spur of the moment, taking into account the uniqueness of the present situation, awareness of previous occasions and discussions, and sensitivity to the personality and circumstances of the pupil(s) and of whoever may be listening or watching.

The material on the next few pages gives general guidance.

Box 37

Closed and open views of the other

Distinctions	Closed views of the other	Open views of the other
1. Monolithic/diverse	The other seen as a single monolithic bloc, static and unresponsive to new realities	The other seen as diverse and progressive, with internal differences, debates and development
2. Separate/interacting	The other seen as separate – (a) not having any aims or values in common with the self; (b) not affected by it; (c) not influencing it	The other seen as interdependent with the self – (a) having certain shared values and aims; (b) affected by it; (c) enriching it
3. Inferior/different	The other seen as inferior to the self – e.g. barbaric, irrational, 'fundamentalist'	The other seen as different from the self but of equal worth
4. Enemy/partner	The other seen as violent, aggressive, threatening, to be defeated and perhaps dominated	The other seen as an actual or potential partner in joint co-operative enterprises and in the solution of shared problems
5. Manipulative/sincere	The other seen as manipulative and deceitful, bent only on material or strategic advantage	The other seen as sincere in their beliefs, not hypocritical
6. Criticisms of the self rejected/considered	Criticisms made by the other of the self are rejected out of hand	Criticisms of the self are considered and debated
7. Discrimination defended/criticised	Hostility towards the other is used to justify discriminatory practices and exclusion of the other from mainstream society	Debates and disagreements with the other do not diminish efforts to combat discrimination and exclusion
8. Hostility towards the other seen as natural/problematic	Fear and hostility towards the other are accepted as natural and 'normal'	Critical views of the other are themselves subjected to critique, lest they be inaccurate and unfair

Box 38

IMAGES AND IMPRESSIONS OF OFSTED

How do teachers see and feel about OFSTED – what is the picture of it in their mind's eye?

Here are some things people say, arranged in pairs.

Please indicate your own views by putting circles in the columns below. If you agree with the statement on the left, then circle one of the figures (3,2 or 1) to the left of the page – the more you agree with it, the further to the left your view will be. If your views are closer to the statement on the right, then similarly please put a circle on the right of the page.

They're all the same, static, unresponsive to change, a monolithic bloc	3	2	1	0	1	2	3	Diverse and progressive, with internal differences, debates and development
They're separate – have different values and aims; are not affected by teachers; do not affect teachers' values.	3	2	1	0	1	2	3	Interdependent with teachers – have certain shared values and aims; are influenced by teachers; enrich teachers' values.
Inferior to teachers	3	2	1	0	1	2	3	Different, but of equal worth
Aggressive, threatening – an enemy to be disarmed and if necessary deceived	3	2	1	0	1	2	3	An actual or potential partner in a joint co-operative enterprise
Manipulative and deceitful	3	2	1	0	1	2	3	Sincere and trustworthy
Any criticisms they make of teachers to be rejected	3	2	1	0	1	2	3	Criticisms of teachers to be considered and debated
Differential treatment of inspectors is acceptable	3	2	1	0	1	2	3	Disagreement is not an excuse for treating inspectors badly
Hostility towards OFSTED entirely natural and normal	3	2	1	0	1	2	3	Critical views of OFSTED are themselves subjected to critique

Box 39

Citizenship education revisited

Knowledge and understanding

Pupils should learn about:

- the origins, implications and changing nature of identities in the United Kingdom, including national (English, Irish, Scottish, Welsh), regional (for example Birmingham, Bradford, Glasgow, Liverpool, London, Manchester...), religious (including British Muslim) and ethnic (including black British, British Asian)

- the development of Britain as a community of communities, in the past as well as today, and the idea that each city and neighbourhood is such a community

- the ways in which Britain is, and always has been, interdependent with the wider world – economic, political, cultural and ecological

- the world as a global community and the need for debate and decision-making at supra-national levels; the role of the European Union, the Commonwealth and the United Nations

- the nature and consequences of racism in society and of racist abuse, bullying and aggressive behaviour in pupils' own experience; how to respond to racist incidents and ask for help; how to challenge them assertively

- the strategies that individuals and voluntary, community and pressure groups use to bring about change locally, nationally, in Europe and internationally, particularly in projects that involve people from different backgrounds working together collaboratively

- similarities between people; shared needs, values and aspirations; shared futures; and differences of narrative, outlook and sense of identity relating to culture, ethnicity, race and religion, and gender and disability

- what improves and what harms the natural and built environments, locally, nationally and internationally; and measures of sustainable development to protect and conserve the environment.

Skills and abilities

Pupils need to develop skills in:

- justifying orally and in writing their personal opinions about issues, problems and events, and contributing to exploratory discussions and debates, showing respect for opinions with which they disagree

- using their imagination to consider other people's experiences and perceptions and being able to think about, express, explain and evaluate views that are not their own

- challenging offensive behaviour, prejudice, bullying, racism and discrimination assertively; taking the initiative in giving and receiving support; helping to mediate in disputes amongst peers

- dealing with changing relationships in a positive way, showing goodwill to others and using strategies to resolve disagreements peacefully

- recognising and challenging stereotypes

- considering critically how events and groups are presented in the media.

Attitudes and feelings

Pupils should develop:

- pride in their own identity and in the communities to which they belong

- readiness to look critically at the various communities to which they belong and to contribute positively to change and improvement

- attitudes of curiosity and generosity towards other identities and communities.

Pastoral concern

At times of great trauma and stress, as on 11 September 2001 and in ensuing weeks, a key task for adults is to provide reassurance, and to help children and young people cope. Counsellors and experienced teachers throughout the world have offered advice on various websites. Some of the simplest and wisest of these documents have been written by Dr Judy Myers-Walls at Purdue University in Indiana. 'Hope,' she says, 'is one of the most valuable gifts we can give children and ourselves'. The pastoral task is to listen and sympathise and to nurture hope and resilience even at times of great distress. There is an edited copy of one of her papers in Box 40. It was sent to all Oakwell schools on the afternoon of 11 September 2001.

Fostering understanding

The fundamental educational task is to help pupils think for themselves and to sort out and clarify their emotions and values. They therefore need skills in weighing up evidence, choosing between alternatives, thinking about pros and cons, showing respect for people with whom they disagree, and abiding by rules and conventions of courtesy and civil argument. So it often helps to turn pupils' questions round – 'What do you think?' 'Why?' Have you always thought that?' 'Are there other ways of seeing this?' 'What do you think might cause you to change or modify your mind?' Distinctions between open and closed views of the other (see Box 37) are relevant in such discussions.

It is miseducation or even indoctrination to say or imply that there is consensus around certain issues when in fact there is not. In national society as in world society there are substantial differences of values, policies and agendas. It can be reassuring to children and young people, rather than merely alarming or depressing, to be reminded that their elders disagree with each other about important matters. It may be more important for them to live with differences and uncertainties than to settle for over-simple solutions.

However, there are certain fundamental moral principles enshrined in national law and international human rights standards. Discrimination on grounds of race or gender is unlawful, for example, and torture and cruelty are widely condemned as unacceptable. It is entirely appropriate for teachers and other adults to assert and stress the values in, for example, the Universal

Declaration on Human Rights, even though there are legitimate disagreements about what the rights involve in practice, and how competing rights are to be balanced.

Protection

Freedom of thought and expression is an important value and should be protected in schools as in wider society. But it is not an absolute value. It can conflict with the equally important right not to be threatened or abused. In practice, the law of the land often puts the right of a person to live in peace and security higher than the right of another person to express their views in insulting and threatening ways. This is usually appropriate in schools as well. Particularly schools have a duty to protect pupils who are vulnerable to hate crimes on the streets and to racist taunts and bullying in the playground. There is fuller discussion of racism, and of ways of preventing and addressing racism in schools, in the next chapter.

Box 40

Talking at times of tragedy

Don't assume children don't know

They probably know more than you think. The reality of today's world is that news travels far and wide. Adults and children learn about disasters and tragedies shortly after they occur, and live video footage with close-ups and interviews are part of the report. Children are exposed to world events as soon as they can watch TV. Not talking about tragedies doesn't protect children. If you remain silent you may communicate that the subject is taboo and that you yourself are not available.

Be available and 'askable'

Let them know that it is okay to talk about unpleasant events. Listen to what they think and feel. By listening, you can find out if they have misunderstandings and learn more about the support they need. You do not need to explain more than they are ready to hear, but be willing to answer their questions.

Share your own feelings

Tell young people if you feel afraid, angry or frustrated. It can help them to know that others are upset. Otherwise they might feel that only children are struggling. If you tell them about your feelings, you can also say how you deal with them. Be careful not to overwhelm children, though, and don't expect them to find answers for you.

Help children use creative outlets like art and music

Children may not be comfortable or skilled with words, especially in relation to difficult situations. Using art, puppets, music or books can help them open up about their reactions. They may want to draw pictures and then destroy them, or they may want to display them or send them to someone else. Be flexible and listen.

Reassure young people and help them feel safe

When tragic events occur, children may be afraid that the same will happen to them. Some may even think that it has happened to them. It is important to let them know that they are not at risk. Try to be realistic as you

reassure them, however. You can try to support them and protect them, but you cannot keep all bad things from happening to them.

Support children's concern for people they do not know

Children are often afraid not only for themselves but also for people they do not even know. They worry about those people and their well being and may feel less secure or cared for themselves if they see that others are hurting. It is heartwarming and satisfying to observe this level of caring in children. Be careful not to encourage the kind of response given by one child: 'I don't care if there's a war, as long as it doesn't affect me and my family.'

Avoid stereotyping

Children may be keen to draw distinctions between good guys and bad guys. Help them to make moral judgements that avoid blanket generalisations about all members of a nation, religion or ethnic group.

Help children find a course of action

One important way to reduce stress is to take action. This is true both for adults and for children. The action may be very simple or more complex. For example, children may want to write a letter to someone about their feelings, or get involved in an organisation committed to preventing events like the one they are dealing with, or send money to help victims or campaigners. Let them help to identify the choices. They may have wonderful ideas.

Take action yourself

It is not enough to let children take action by themselves. If they know that their parents, teachers or other significant adults are working to make a difference they will feel hope and safer and more positive about the future. So do something. It will make you feel more hopeful, too. Hope at times of tragedy is one of the most valuable gifts we can give children and ourselves.

Source: adapted from guidance issued from Purdue

6 Dealing with racisms
– preventing and addressing racism in its various forms

What was there to say?

In his book *No Place Like Home*, Gary Younge recalls a trip to the seaside with a community organisation when he was about twelve years old. A bus was hired and all the passengers were black – mainly children, but also some parents and leaders. 'I was sitting on my own by a window,' writes Younge, 'reading a book, when the coach stopped at traffic lights... On the other side of the road about six skinheads – shaved scalps, bleached jeans at half mast, thin Lonsdale T-shirts and eighteen hole Doctor Marten boots – were walking in the opposite direction carrying cans of cheap beer, when one of them spotted us, a bus full of black kids aged roughly between eight and fourteen, dressed up for a day out and stuck on a red light.'

The episode that followed has stayed with Younge, he says, all his life. 'By the time they reached the middle of the road they had started chanting "Nigger... Nigger... Nigger, Nigger, Nigger." ... Within seconds the crowd on the bus had gone from boisterous kids about to get dropped off at the seaside to a bustling, yelling house of panic on four wheels. The smaller children were starting to scream... The skinheads were upon us, bashing on the window, shouting "Nigger" and trying to rock the coach. The look on their faces was not one of hate but sport. We felt terrified and they were enjoying themselves.'

Younge comments: 'After that it was never mentioned again. What was there to say, and who would you say it to anyway?'

For schools, the episode raises three sets of issues:

- How to ensure that children on the receiving end of verbal and physical racism have someone to tell about their stories and experiences, so that they can receive support and solidarity

- How to deal with the offenders

- How to prevent episodes of racism occurring in the first place.

These are the questions addressed in this chapter. An essential preliminary question is to do with understanding and defining racism. Accordingly the chapter begins with materials for inservice training activities that help to clarify the concept.

Clarifying key distinctions and concepts

The first activity outlined here is entitled 'Racism over the decades'. Participants work in twos or threes, and each group is given a set of ten quotations on separate slips of paper or cards. They are informed that each quotation comes from a different decade since 1900 and are asked to arrange them in chronological order. Box 41 shows quotations that were used in Oakwell. (The dates and sources are given in Box 41 but these need to be removed for the exercise itself.)

The value of the exercise lies in the discussion that it promotes within the small groups and in the way it encourages a historical overview and a spirit of study and reflection. The participants literally handle the ideas, and this symbolises that they are in control of their own learning and are free to make preliminary sense of the material in their own way. A conventional talk or lecture on the same subject-matter would probably be threatening and intimidating for several participants. But if participants feel they are in control, they are more likely to engage with the issues and to develop intellectual understanding. Such understanding will then underpin their resolve to address the three questions listed above – supporting those who are attacked, dealing with offenders and striving to prevent racist behaviour from occurring in the first place.

The next stage is to consider matters of definition and description. Three possible exercises are shown in Boxes 42, 43 and 44. The first involves looking at some extracts from a remarkable book written by a French author of Moroccan background, Tahar Ben Jelloun, whose ten-year-old daughter asked him one day to explain to her what racism is, and who pressed him then with a series of further questions over the following days and weeks. Eventually he wrote down her questions and his answers, and in their written form these were discussed and clarified with the girl's friends. Some extracts are shown in Box 42. They give a flavour of the style and approach, but definitely are not a summary.

An inservice activity with UK teachers based on Jelloun's book can have three stages:

- First, participants are given the questions in Box 42 and asked to write brief answers for ten-year-old children.

Box 41

Aspects of racism over the years

Only a matter of time

It is only a matter of time before the population becomes entirely foreign. The rates are burdened with the education of thousands of children of foreign parents. Among the thousands who come here there is a considerable proportion of bad characters, and the competition with home industries extends to burglary and other cognate crimes. (Evans Gordon MP, 1902)

Black face

Here is a native who has actually behaved like a gentleman; if it was not for his black face we would almost allow him to join the club. (E.M.Forster's A Passage to India, 1920s)

Modern civilised life

It is to European man that the world owes the incomparable gifts of modern science. To the conquest of nature through knowledge the contributions made by Asiatics have been negligible and by Africans (Egyptians excluded) non-existent. It is hardly excessive to say that the material fabric of modern civilised life is the result of the intellectual daring and tenacity of the European peoples. (H.A.L Fisher, A History of Europe, 1930s)

Squalid and deplorable

Most live in housing conditions that are primitive, squalid and deplorable. Many police reports say that coloured people seem to live in these bad conditions from choice. West Indian men are physically unsuited for heavy manual work and are volatile and potentially violent, and the women are slow mentally. Indians are mainly hardworking though unscrupulous. (Home Office report, 1950s)

Neighbour

If you want a nigger neighbour, vote Labour. (Election campaign slogan in Smethwick, 1960s)

Tale of talent

Too often the history of Europe is described as a series of interminable wars and quarrels. Yet from our perspective today surely what strikes us most is our common experience. For instance, the story of how Europeans explored and colonised and – yes – civilised much of the world is an extraordinary tale of talent, skill and courage. (Margaret Thatcher, 1980s)

Walking down the street

I still don't feel British. Because I know we haven't been fully accepted. We still walk down the street and get called a Paki. (Focus group, 1999)

Going to die

It won't be long before Christianity is dead and buried and Britain becomes an Islamic dictatorship. After all, what can stop them? With continued immigration, high birthrates and conversions to Islam, Christianity is being crucified on the dark cross of multiculturalism and globalisation... Unless we change things Christianity in Britain is going to die. And senior church leaders are queuing up to be the grave-diggers ... (British National Party, 2001)

Box 42

Racism explained to a child

Daddy, what is racism?

Racism is a common phenomenon that occurs in every society. Unfortunately, it has become quite common in certain countries, where it exists without anyone even thinking about it. It consists of being mistrustful of people, and even of looking down on those who have physical and cultural characteristics different from your own.

If it's universal, could I be racist?

Well, children aren't usually racist by nature. No one is born racist. If your parents or the people around you don't put racist ideas in your head, there's no reason you should become so. But if you're led to believe that people with white skin are superior to people with dark skin, and if you take this idea seriously, you might have a racist attitude towards black people.

Daddy, people talk about the white race, the black race, the yellow race. We hear that at school. The teacher told us the other day that Abdou's race is black. He's from Mali.

If your teacher really said that, she was wrong. I hate to tell you this, because I know you like her, but she's wrong ... Human races don't exist. There is a human species in which there are men and women, people of color, tall people and short people, with different strengths and weaknesses ... The word 'race' has no scientific basis ... We shouldn't use physical differences – skin color, height, facial features – to divide humanity hierarchically. That is, to claim that some people are better than others.

So what can we do?

We can learn, we can educate ourselves and we can think. We can try to understand things, to be curious about everything that affects people, to control our instincts and impulses.

...We must do what we can to fight against racism every single day. We cannot allow ourselves to become complacent. We can begin by setting a good example to others; always paying attention to the words we use. Words can be dangerous. They can be used to hurt and humiliate people, to create hatred and mistrust ...

...When you go back to school, look at all the other pupils. Notice how different they all are, how wonderful this diversity is ... Every face is unique, a miracle ... Every face symbolises a life and every life deserves respect. No one has the right to humiliate another human being. Everyone has the right to dignity. By respecting others we honour life in all its beauty, magic, diversity and unpredictability. Respecting others allows us to respect ourselves.

Source: these are extracts from *Racism Explained To My Daughter* by Tahar Ben Jelloun, originally published in France as *Le racisme expliqué à ma fille* in 1999. The English translation is published by The New Press, New York.

Box 43

Definitions of racism

Racism in general terms consists of conduct or words or practices which disadvantage or advantage people because of their colour, culture or ethnic origin. In its more subtle form it is as damaging as in its overt form. (*Stephen Lawrence Inquiry report,* 1999)

A belief in the superiority of a particular race; prejudice and antagonism based on this; the theory that human abilities etc are determined by race. (*Oxford English Dictionary,* slightly adapted)

Racism is a common phenomenon that occurs in every society. It consists of being mistrustful of people, and even of looking down on those who have physical and cultural characteristics different from your own. (Tahar Ben Jelloun, *Racism Explained to My Daughter,* 2000)

The term racism summarises all attitudes, procedures and social patterns whose effect (though not necessarily whose conscious intention) is to create and maintain the power, influence and well-being of white people at the expense of Asian and African-Caribbean people; and whose further function is simultaneously to limit the latter to the poorest life chances and living conditions, the most menial work, and the greatest likelihood of unemployment and under-employment. (Berkshire Education Authority, quoted in the *Swann report,* 1985)

[Racism] is a complex of attitudes, actions, beliefs and structures, at personal, communal and institutional levels ... It arises as a distorted expression of positive human needs, especially for belonging, identity and free expression of difference and is expressed in destructive patterns of relating: hardening the boundaries between groups; overlooking others; belittling, dehumanising or demonising others; justifying or collaborating in the domination of others; physically intimidating or attacking others. (The Corrymeela Community, Northern Ireland, 2001, slightly adapted)

- Second, they compare their own answers with those of Tahar Ben Jelloun.

- Third, they devise up to three further questions that might be asked by children in British contexts, and draft their written answers.

Instead of using the material by Tahar Ben Jelloun, or in addition to it, it is valuable to consider definitions of racism in writings for adults. There are four such definitions in Box 43, plus also the one provided by Jelloun.

A further way of beginning to grapple with the complexity of racism is illustrated in Box 44. The material here is based on a paragraph in *The Future of Multi-Ethnic Britain*. It consists of a succinct summary of one of the most important facets of racism – the interaction of physical and cultural factors. It is formatted as a cloze procedure exercise. Working in pairs, participants decide through discussion what the missing words should be. Then in fours or sixes they compare and contrast their proposals and try to reach consensus. The activity enables them to internalise the key distinction between 'colour racism' and 'cultural racism' in a way that a formal talk or lecture is unlikely to do.

The plurality of racism

At the World Conference Against Racism (WCAR) held in South Africa in 2001, it was agreed that the term 'racism' is a shorthand way of referring to a set of realities that cannot be adequately named with a single word. The full phrase that the WCAR adopted was 'racism, racial discrimination, xenophobia, intolerance and related phenomena'. An alternative way of shortening the full phrase is to use the plural term 'racisms', as in the title of this chapter.

The plural term is ugly but it stresses that there are several key distinctions which must be recognised and worked with. Five such distinctions are noted below.

First, racism takes different forms according to those who are targeted and what their characteristics are believed to be. For example, anti-Black racism is different from anti-Asian racism, and both are different from anti-Muslim racism, also known as Islamophobia. Also anti-Irish racism must be recognised, and anti-Jewish racism and anti-Gypsy racism. Latterly, there has

Box 44

Two strands in all racisms

Over the centuries all racisms have had – and continue to have – two separate but _____ strands.

One uses _____ or biologically derived signs as a way of recognising difference – skin colour, hair, features, body type, and so on. The other uses _____ features, such as ways of life, customs, language, religion and dress. The two strands usually appear together, but they combine in distinct ways, with one or other _____ at different times and in different contexts.

Jews were vilified in medieval times because they were believed to be the _____ of Christ, and because they practised a strict but alien code of _____ law and social behaviour. But they also came to be represented as _____ different – with hooked nose, ringlets and a swarthy complexion. In the antisemitic iconography of Nazi Germany they were consistently portrayed as _____. Similarly Gypsies have been discriminated against because of both their _____ lifestyle and their 'non-Caucasian' physical appearance. In the nineteenth century the Irish, who had always been regarded by the British as less _____, were racialised – represented in the press and popular cartoons as ape-like, a race apart.

In addition to Jews, Gypsies and the Irish in Europe, the targets of racism over the centuries have included peoples and civilisations beyond Europe's boundaries, including, of course, the _____ peoples.

The missing words in Box 44 are intertwining, physical, cultural, prominent, murderers, dietary, physically, subhuman, nomadic, civilised, colonised.

emerged in Britain and Ireland, and indeed throughout western Europe, a set of phenomena which can be described as anti-refugee racism.

Second, a distinction must be drawn between the biological strand in each racism and the cultural strand. Both are almost always present, but in different combinations at different times and in different places. The biological strand uses physical features of supposed difference, particularly skin colour and facial features, to recognise 'the other'. The cultural strand refers to differences of religion, language and way of life. Both strands involve believing that certain differences amongst human beings are fixed as well as significant, can justify unjust distributions of power and resources, and can determine who is and who is not a full or real member of the national society. The distinction is sometimes said to be between 'colour racism' and 'cultural racism', or between North-South racism and West-East racism. Such phrases have their uses but obscure the reality that physical and cultural markers are usually combined.

Since there is always a cultural strand in racism, it is important to stress not only equality as a core value but also recognition of cultural difference and the importance of social cohesion. (See the discussions of these points in Chapter 1 and Chapter 5, and the references to cultural diversity and social cohesion in the specimen school policy statement later in this chapter.)

Third, it is frequently useful to distinguish between attitudes and assumptions on the one hand and personal and institutional behaviour on the other. The one reference is to the explanatory stories which people tell and the big pictures in their minds' eyes – for example, the stories and pictures shown in Box 41 (Aspects of racism over the years). The other refers to what people do and don't do, in their customs and manners as well as their actions.

The relationship between attitudes and behaviour is two-way. It is not necessarily the case that people first form attitudes and then act in accordance with them. Sometimes they adopt certain behaviour first and then develop attitudes to justify it. Either way, attitudes are frequently expressed through and in stories – grand narratives about the nation and its history, as recalled in Chapter 5, and various anecdotes from local affairs and personal memory.

Fourth, racism is gendered. Women of all ethnicities are affected by it in not quite the same ways as men. When race equality and gender equality initiatives are pursued independently of each other, the principal beneficiaries are respectively Asian and black men on the one hand and white women on the other. Further, all so-called racial relationships are affected by sexual rivalries, sexual fantasies and currents of sexual attraction.

Fifth, it is crucial to distinguish between institutional racism and street racism. Another formulation of this distinction refers to 'the racism that discriminates' and 'the racism that kills'. A solution to the one is seldom a solution to the other – though they are certainly connected in various ways, not two entirely different beasts. Institutional racism is to do with the way an institution treats people, regardless of the intentions and conscious awareness of its members. Also, it is to do with taken-for-granted assumptions and common sense in an organisation's culture. These two points about the net effect of an institution and the occupational culture of its members were well put to the Stephen Lawrence Inquiry by representatives of the Black Police Association and are quoted in Box 45. At an inservice

training course for teachers it is relevant to consider the ways in which the occupational culture in school staff rooms is similar or analogous to the occupational culture of the police service. The material in Boxes 12 and 13 can valuably inform such discussion. See also the account in Chapter 4 of teachers' mental maps and 'inner eyes', and the ways these affect their expectations of individual pupils and groups of pupils. Tackling institutional racism in education necessarily involves critical review of the taken-for-granted assumptions in staffroom cultures.

The term 'street racism', as distinct from 'institutional racism', refers to overt aggressive acts. Such acts exist on a continuum of seriousness. At one end of the continuum are major crimes of violence, for example the murder of Stephen Lawrence. At the other end there is wordless and careless discourtesy. In between, there are verbal remarks and acts of vandalism. Acts that are less serious from a legal point of view can nevertheless be extremely distressing for those who are attacked and for their friends, contacts and family. The metaphor of street captures the fact that such behaviour usually takes place in public spaces.

Box 45

Occupational cultures and net effects

The term institutional racism should be understood to refer to the way an institution or organisation may systematically or repeatedly treat, or tend to treat, people differently because of their race. So ... we are not talking about individuals in the service, who may be unconscious as to the nature of what they are doing, but about the net effect of what they do.

A second source of institutional racism is our culture ... How and why does that impact on black individuals on the street? Well, we would say the occupational culture within the police service, given the fact that the majority of police officers are white, tends to be the white experience, the white beliefs, the white values.

Given that these predominantly white officers only meet members of the black community in confrontational situations, they tend to stereotype black people in general. This can lead to all sorts of negative views and assumptions about black people, so we should not underestimate the occupational culture within the police service as being a primary source of institutional racism in the way we differentially treat black people.

Interestingly I say we because there is no marked difference between black and white in the force essentially. We are all consumed by this occupational culture. Some of us may think we rise above it on some occasions, but generally speaking we tend to conform to the norms of the occupational culture, [for it's] ... all powerful in shaping our views and perceptions of a particular community.

Source: oral evidence from the Metropolitan Police Service Black Police Association to the Stephen Lawrence Inquiry, 1998.

Many acts of street racism are perpetrated by children and young people of school-age or aged 17-21. So schools have essential responsibilities in addressing racism and preventing it. This was stressed in the Stephen Lawrence Inquiry report, and Ofsted now has a formal responsibility to inspect and to report on how schools and local authorities address overt racism amongst pupils. It follows that schools have to be aware of street racism in their vicinity. But their actual sphere of responsibility is necessarily more limited. A term such as 'playground racism' is therefore appropriate. Again, this is a metaphor. It refers to the spaces in a school where pupils interact without being directly supervised by adults – the spaces where the streets outside the school penetrate the school itself. There is fuller discussion below.

Playground racism

In the mid 1990s the Home Office funded research into overt racism. The principal points to emerge, so far as schools are concerned, were that playground racism must be seen as part of playground culture, not just the behaviour of lone individuals; that playground culture is integrally related to street culture; and that street culture, particularly for younger age groups, is intimately linked to the culture of certain homes and families. These points were stressed through the compilation of offender profiles and are illustrated in Box 46. They have substantial implications for how incidents of playground racism are dealt with and for the efforts a school takes to prevent racist incidents occurring in the first place.

The research noted that teachers have available to them four main strategies:

• ignoring

• disapproval

• intellectual argument

• adopting a holistic approach.

There are further notes of these below, based on the researchers' findings.

Ignoring or making light of the incident

This is seldom if ever appropriate. It permits the offender – and the offender's friends and associates – to assume that there is nothing wrong with their behaviour,

Racist incidents – profiles of offenders

Box 46

Primary school age

Racism is part of the language with which offenders have grown up – grandparents, parents and elder siblings hold, and regularly express, racist views. The recurring notion is that people who are not white 'do not belong here' and 'should go back where they came from'. It is considered normal to hold this view and to voice it to others without fear of contradiction.

At school they may be bullies, and may do their best to avoid co-operating, working or sitting with Asian and black classmates – particularly if they can do this without being noticed by their teachers.

They seldom move far from their home and neighbourhood, and in this sense have narrow horizons – they are unfamiliar even with the city where they live, let alone with the countryside or with other countries.

They see racist harassment as a sport or pastime, particularly during the school holidays when there's not much else to do, and when they are travelling between home and school.

Secondary school age range

They are likely to be low achievers, as also probably were their parents, and generally feel that the school does not care about them. In order to achieve a certain self-esteem and gain respect and prestige in the teenage peer group, they are likely to bully anyone they see as weaker than themselves. If those they pick on are Asian or black, they are likely to justify their behaviour in racist terms.

They engage in continual harassment of local families, particularly if there's a chance in this way of impressing older youths, and are abusive and threatening towards people they pass on the street, particularly those who are strangers in their neighbourhood.

They may well have black or Asian friends at school. But they see no inconsistency between this and their racism. They do not mix with Asian or black people out of school, or after they have left school.

They may engage in physical assaults and violence.

Source: adapted from *The Perpetrators of Racial Harassment and Racial Violence*, Home Office Research Study 176, 1997.

so they may repeat it. Also, this approach gives no support to the pupils who have been attacked. They may in consequence assume their teachers and the school generally are indifferent to racism and they will see no point in reporting further incidents.

Disapproval

This is sometimes entirely appropriate. The offender and any onlookers must be in no doubt that the behaviour is unacceptable, and any pupil who has been attacked must be in no doubt that they are supported by the school. But if rebukes and punishments are not complemented by teaching and learning about why racism is wrong, punishment may merely feed pupils' bitterness and sense of not being understood. Such bitterness may then be expressed elsewhere, out of the school's domain.

Intellectual argument

It is important that teachers and youth workers explain why racism is wrong and demonstrate with facts and rationality that racist beliefs are both false and harmful. This may involve pointing out that even when a factual statement is true ('They own all the corner shops round here') it does not justify violence or hatred. But like rebukes and punishments, intellectual arguments may merely feed bitterness and a sense of not being understood. If offenders then feel an increased sense of personal inferiority and powerlessness and greater resentment of authority, they may become more racist in their attitudes and behaviour rather than less.

A holistic approach

Racist beliefs and behaviour in young people have their sources in anxieties about identity and territory and in desires to belong to a sub-culture of peers or a gang where racism is one (but usually not the only one) of the defining features. Teachers and youth workers should show that they understand such anxieties, desires and peer pressures and should try to engage with them. If this approach is to be effective, it needs to be accompanied by a range of other, more specific measures and strategies. Such measures and strategies have to involve all pupils, not just those who have engaged in racist behaviour or made racist remarks.

The Home Office research concluded that a distinction should be drawn between (a) actual offenders (b) potential offenders and (c) 'the offender community' – friends, contacts and families of actual or potential offenders. It suggested that these three groups could be visualised as three circles, as shown in Figure 3, and stressed that the tasks of addressing and preventing racism in schools and youth clubs should involve all three groups.

Figure 3: Offenders and the offender community

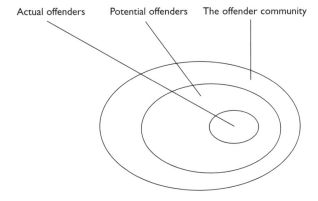

Actual offenders   Potential offenders   The offender community

---

Box 47

Playground racism

The distinctive feature of a racist incident is that a person is attacked not as an individual, as in most other offences, but as the _____ of a community. This has three particularly serious consequences.

- Other members of the same _____ are made to feel threatened and _____ as well, and are less inclined to venture into public spaces. So it is not just the person who is attacked who suffers a _____ of his or her freedom and security.

- Since racist attacks affect a _____ as well as an individual, they are experienced as attacks on the values, _____ and commitments central to a person's sense of _____ and self-worth – their family honour, friends, culture, heritage, _____, community, history. Racist, cultural and religious abuse is accordingly more _____ than most other kinds of abuse.

- Racist attacks are committed not only against a community but also, in the _____ of offenders themselves, on behalf of a community – offenders see themselves as representative of, and supported in their racism by, their friends, family and peer group. Even more than in the case of most other offences, it is therefore essential that a school should clearly show _____ with and support for those who are targeted, and take care not to provide any kind of comfort or _____ to the offenders, or to the _____ to which they see themselves as belonging.

The missing words in Box 47 are representative, community, insecure, curtailment, community, loyalties, identity, religion, hurtful, perception, solidarity, encouragement, community.

Dealing with incidents

It is essential that teachers and administrative staff should be clear, both collectively and as individuals, about why racist incidents are even more serious than other kinds of bullying and aggressive behaviour amongst pupils. Such clarity comes not only from formal statements in the staff handbook but also from reflective discussion. One way to promote such discussion is to use the material in Box 47. It is adapted from a paragraph in *The Future of Multi-Ethnic Britain* and again involves a cloze procedure. Participants work first in pairs then in fours. The processes of discussing and choosing between appropriate terms help them to internalise the key points.

Following up a racist incident is sensitive and can be difficult for everybody involved. It is made easier for all in a school with the following features.

- The entire school community is aware of and understands the school's values and principles in respect of equality

- The entire school community is aware of procedures for reporting and dealing with racist incidents, and of roles and responsibilities associated with them

- Pupils feel safe to report incidents, whether as witnesses or having been targeted

- There is a history of taking reports seriously and following them up

- Issues of racism, prejudice and bullying are routinely and openly discussed within the school community, and especially with pupils, and such discussion is an integral part of the overall school curriculum

- Pupils themselves are involved in dealing with racist incidents, when appropriate, for example through peer mediation processes.

Where these conditions apply, the pupils will already have a shared dialogue and discourse with adults and will be able to name and describe what has happened. The respective responsibilities of all members of the school community are tabulated in Box 48.

When dealing with cases of racist bullying and harassment, it is important to take account of the following points:

- Being subjected to racist bullying and harassment is traumatic. The pupil who has been attacked is likely to be distressed and angry. He or she may suffer from the effects long after the actual incident.

- Care should be taken when deciding who the investigating and supporting adults should be. For example, it may be valuable to designate an adult who already has a relationship with the pupil, and to consider whether they have been trained or have special skills and responsibilities, and whether they have in common with the pupil their ethnicity, culture, gender, religion or language. This is not to say that all these features need to be present in all cases but rather that they could be important in some circumstances.

- The wider context and effects should not be forgotten. Verbal abuse directed at one pupil will distress pupils who belong to the same community, especially those who witness it.

- It is important that the pupil who has been attacked is kept informed of what is happening as a result of the report. He or she may request that no action be taken, in fear of reprisals. If the incident has been reported by a witness, the pupil who has been attacked may need to be reassured that there will be no reprisals, and that he or she will be supported by staff and peers.

- Even the youngest children can be affected. It is a fallacy to suppose that children in the nursery 'do not notice colour' – they do, and they can hurt and be hurt by racist language and behaviour. Further, it is essential that children do not learn at an early age that adults find racist behaviour acceptable.

Box 48

The school as an antiracist community

All members of the school community have a responsibility and a role in preventing and addressing racist incidents, as shown in the tabulation below.

MEMBERS OF THE SCHOOL COMMUNITY	ROLE IN DEALING WITH RACIST INCIDENTS
All pupils	Taking responsibility for promoting a harmonious school community; challenging racist behaviour; mediating in disputes; reporting racism to staff; supporting pupils who are attacked.
All teachers	Challenging racist behaviour as soon as it arises; following it up as appropriate; upholding race equality policies; promoting a school atmosphere and ethos stressing equality and inclusion.
All parents	Accepting the school race equality policies; ensuring their children understand and adhere to them; reporting racist incidents to school; supporting those who are attacked.
All governors	Taking a lead in addressing racist incidents; ensuring that the policies and procedures are in place; reporting annually to the LEA.
Headteacher	Promoting a school atmosphere and ethos where all pupils are valued and where diversity is acknowledged as a positive asset; ensuring pupils from all backgrounds have equal access to the curriculum; ensuring equality policies are in place and are understood and implemented by everyone; ensuring procedures for recording, reporting and dealing with racist incidents are embedded in the school processes; reporting to governors on racist incidents; ensuring that all staff have an understanding of racism and good practice in dealing with instances of it
Class teachers and form tutors	Promoting an appropriate classroom atmosphere; challenging racist behaviour; supporting pupils who have been targeted; making sure that offenders are dealt with and followed up over a period of time.
Staff with pastoral responsibility	Taking a lead in developing appropriate support and discipline procedures and policies.
All classroom assistants, adminstrative staff, caretakers	Being vigilant at all times and intervening and challenging incidents if seen. In classrooms and playground, being ready to listen to pupils who have been attacked and take their reports seriously. Supporting distressed pupils; reporting incidents to the headteacher or a designated staff member; removing graffiti.
Mentors	If mentoring a pupil who has been a target of racism, offering support, rebuilding confidence and self-esteem, listening. If mentoring an offender, working to change attitude and behaviour.
Parents of offender	Taking responsibility to support the school's policies and ensuring that the son or daughter is taught appropriate behaviour
Parents of pupils who are targeted	Ensuring that any incident is reported; supporting the child and keeping in touch with the school to share information and be part of a co-ordinated programme of support.

Recording and reporting

In common with most other local education authorities Oakwell has issued guidance on recording and reporting racist incidents in schools. In conversations and consultations with headteachers it has found that the guidance needs to be accompanied by a set of FAQs – frequently asked questions. The notes below show how the questions in Oakwell were phrased and answered.

Why are we doing this?

- Schools and LEAs have a statutory duty to report information on racist incidents to the government. This has arisen from the Home Secretary's recommendations following the Stephen Lawrence Inquiry. The purpose of such reporting is to monitor the level of racist incidents nationally and regionally, to look for any patterns in their occurrence and to plan steps to prevent and address them.

- In Oakwell we wish to collect information that will enable us to establish a baseline, monitor any patterns and use the information to plan and evaluate provision. We will be feeding information back to headteachers and chairs of governors on the progress we are making so that they can compare their own experience with aggregated LEA data, and will consult on any need for action.

- For years schools have recorded instances of bullying and dealt with them. Racist incidents are even more harmful than other kinds of bullying, since they attack communities as well as individuals (see Box 47). Procedures of reporting and recording enable schools to identify and analyse specific types of incident. They contribute to school self-evaluation and action-planning processes, and identify needs which can be picked up through the PSHE and citizenship curriculum as well as through the school pastoral processes.

How will the information be used?

- The information from schools collected by the LEA will be used in aggregated form only. It will be analysed to identify trends and patterns and to monitor and evaluate progress in preventing and addressing racism.

- Information on the ethnicity of offenders and those who are attacked will give us information on any specific needs, possibly arising from changing populations or media reports on a current news item.

- Information on types of incidents recorded will give some indication of the seriousness of incidents in the borough. It will also identify other issues, for example that extremist organisations are distributing racist literature to pupils in schools.

Who will see the information?

- The information will be returned to the LEA in aggregated form. LEA systems will hold the information for aggregation and analysis but without the names of individual schools,. Feedback information to schools will be in aggregated format only. Information submitted to the government will be in the statutory aggregated format, showing numbers of incidents and those where follow-up action has been taken.

- No information on individual schools will be published.

Should schools aim for a nil return?

- A school's population does not exist in a vacuum away from the rest of society, nor is it unchanging. It would be unreasonable in any school to expect that no racist incidents will ever occur. A nil return from a school may indicate that pupils are not confident about reporting incidents, or that staff have not understood the seriousness of such incidents.

Will it look bad if a school has many incidents on its return?

- Absolutely not. On the contrary, recording of incidents is evidence that the school has developed a positive atmosphere and ethos in which pupils feel safe to report incidents to staff.

- If the reporting procedures are effective, an initial increase in the number of incidents reported can be expected, as schools become more successful in promoting this positive ethos. It can be expected that the numbers of reported incidents will subsequently decrease, as schools develop more effective measures for preventing them.

Do we have to record small, insignificant incidents?

• Yes, every incident, no matter how seemingly small, must be recorded and dealt with. Racist name-calling is hurtful and damaging to the pupil who is attacked and to the school community. If offenders are permitted to believe that racism is acceptable they may become involved later in serious criminal violence.

• Recording seemingly minor incidents can be useful to the school, for example in identifying whether current events or local contexts are causing an increase in harassment of particular pupils.

• It is usually possible to deal with minor incidents straightaway, in the classroom or playground context. Only the more serious or repeated incidents will need reporting on to parents or outside agencies.

Could highlighting racist incidents lead to a worse situation?

• It is important to deal with situations sensitively, and therefore to avoid over-reacting or creating martyrs and thus bringing the school rules into disrepute.

• However, far greater danger lies in ignoring incidents and giving pupils the impression that adults condone racist behaviour. Ignoring incidents means that pupils targeted by racism and their friends and families feel unsupported and that offenders feel affirmed and approved of.

How do we decide if an incident is racist?

• As recommended by Ofsted, Oakwell has adopted the definition of a racist incident created by the Association of Chief Police Officers (ACPO) and modified slightly by the Stephen Lawrence Inquiry report: '*Any incident which is perceived to be racist by the victim or any other person*'.

• When an incident perceived to be racist is investigated at a school, the following points should be considered.

    • whether the alleged offender was heard to use racist language at the time of the offence

    • whether the alleged offender is known to hold racist views or to engage in racist behaviour

    • whether the alleged offender is part of a friendship group known to hold racist views or engage in racist behaviour

    • whether the alleged offender is wearing outward signs of belonging to a racist culture (for example, skinhead clothes and haircut, BNP insignia)

    • whether the clothing of the person attacked clearly identified her or him as belonging to a particular religious or cultural group

    • whether there was no, or only slight, provocation

    • whether there is no other explanation for the incident.

Race equality policy statements

In common with many other authorities, Oakwell has provided model policies and guidance to all its schools in connection with the requirements of the Race Relations Amendment Act. One of the models draws on the experience of the Inclusive Classrooms, Inclusive Schools project and is shown in Box 49 in a slightly expanded form. The model is consistent with official guidance issued by the Commission for Racial Equality but also contains some explicit references to cultural and religious diversity as well as equality.

It is important, as shown in Box 49, that the concepts and concerns in a race equality statement should be comprehensive. It is not only the content of a statement, however, that is important. Also important is the process by which a statement is developed. At Broadway High School the process stretched over several years. A key starting point was when the school set up a substantial mentoring scheme for African-Caribbean students at risk of being excluded. The scheme was strikingly successful and received national publicity. It also had the effect of enabling a Black Parents Group to start and prepared the way for a major project run in association with the Windsor Fellowship. Box 50 shows some of its impact.

■ *continued on page 83*

Box 49

Race equality policy statement

1. Legal duties

(Name of school) welcomes its duties under the Race Relations Amendment Act 2000, as also the recommendations to schools in the Stephen Lawrence Inquiry report of 1999. Accordingly we are committed to:

- promoting good relations between members of different racial, cultural and religious groups and communities, and a common sense of belonging

- preventing and addressing racism

- eliminating unlawful discrimination, and promoting equality of opportunity with a view to achieving equality of outcome.

2. Guiding principles

In fulfilling the commitments listed above, we are guided by three essential principles:

- Every pupil should have opportunities to achieve the highest possible standards, and the best possible qualifications for the next stages of their life and education

- Every pupil should be helped to develop a sense of personal and cultural identity that is confident but open to change, and that is receptive and respectful towards other identities

- Every pupil should develop the knowledge, understandings and skills they need for taking responsibility to help Britain flourish as a multi-ethnic democracy, locally as well as nationally and within the wider context of an interdependent world

3. The full range of school policies and practice

We ensure that the principles listed above apply to the full range of our policies and practices, including those that are concerned with pupils' progress, attainment and assessment; behaviour, discipline and exclusions; pupils' personal development and pastoral care; teaching and learning; admissions and attendance; the content of the curriculum; staff recruitment and professional development; and partnerships with parents and communities

4. Addressing racism and xenophobia

The school is opposed to all forms of racism and xenophobia, including those forms that are directed towards religious groups and communities, for example

Islamophobia, and against Travellers, refugees and asylum-seekers.

5. Responsibilities

The governing body is responsible for ensuring that the school complies with legislation, and that this policy and its related procedures and strategies are implemented.

The headteacher is responsible for implementing the policy; for ensuring that all staff are aware of their responsibilities and are given appropriate training and support; and for taking appropriate action in any cases of unlawful discrimination.

All staff are expected to deal with racist incidents that may occur; to know how to identify and challenge racial and cultural bias and stereotyping; to support pupils in their class for whom English is an additional language; and to incorporate principles of equality and diversity into all aspects of their work.

6. Information and resources

We ensure that the content of this policy is known to all staff and governors and, as appropriate, to all pupils and parents.

All staff and governors have access to a selection of resources which discuss and explain concepts of race equality and cultural diversity in appropriate detail.

7. Religious observance

We respect the religious beliefs and practice of all staff, pupils and parents, and comply with all reasonable requests relating to religious observance and practice.

8. Action plan

We draw up an annual action plan for the implementation of this policy and for monitoring its impact.

9. Breaches of the policy

Breaches of this policy will be dealt with in the same ways that breaches of other school policies are dealt with, as determined by the headteacher and governing body.

10. Monitoring and evaluation

We collect, study and use quantitative and qualitative data relating to the implementation of this policy, and make adjustments as appropriate.

Date approved by the Governing Body:

■ *continued from page 81*

Other projects included sessions for school governors, work with African artists, historical research using the Internet during Black History Month, racism awareness training for staff, the piloting of material for *The Life of* *Stephen Lawrence* by Verna Allette Wilkins and a visit to the school by Neville Lawrence. Out of this wide range of activities there emerged in due course the school's race equality policy statement. The process is shown as a flow chart in Figure 4 on page 84.

Box 50

If you reach out to them

What did you do?

A trainer from the Windsor Fellowship worked with a group of 27 Year 10 boys and girls, the majority of them African-Caribbean boys. There were eight sessions at fortnightly intervals. Quite a few of the students had really poor interpersonal skills, often getting into conflict with other students and with teachers and so on. With the trainer from the Windsor Fellowship they worked on group dynamics and how to present themselves. The Fellowship shows them how to handle situations, how you present yourself to people, the perceptions people have of who you are.

What was the impact on the students?

One of the students said they will ask a question to a teacher but they don't get an answer. Also the students said that often staff don't ask them questions – they put their hands up but aren't asked and as a result they shout out and then got told off for doing so. The trainer talked to them about how to ask questions. They found this really enlightening – they'd never thought about it before.

One of the most noticeable aspects was the fact that on the first session there were fourteen students on amber and red reports. But about two or three sessions into the programme there was only one student on amber report.

The trainer was black and they were encouraged to see that they didn't have to limit themselves in what they do when they leave school

What happened next?

We took on the LEA Raising African Caribbean Achievement in Schools project and as part of that Neville Lawrence, Stephen's father, came to the school. And we are now having racism awareness training for the whole staff ... The trainer began by inviting staff to share their experiences of how they perceive themselves, where their grandparents came from, how they were brought up. It made them think about how students feel. I can't be too specific because there was a confidentiality agreement. It helped staff to talk to each other and also staff have felt confident enough to say their concerns. We talked about misunderstandings of certain cultures and about perceptions of black students.

What have you learnt?

First, if you want something strongly enough you have to fight for it.

And I've also learnt from this project that though these students are underachieving and their behaviour is a concern, beneath it all they're still children. If you reach out to them and you talk to them and you give them the chance to talk to one other, and if you challenge them about their behaviour, then you can get something positive out of it. I think it should be done more.

Source: extracts from an interview with a teacher at Broadway High School

Figure 4: Practice into policy: one school's journey

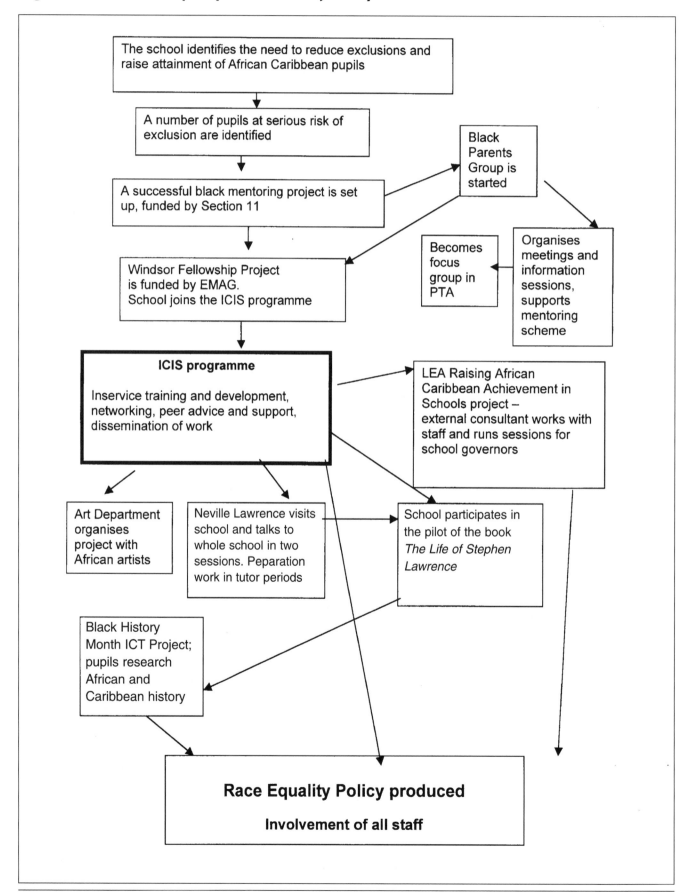

Remembering Stephen Lawrence

The book by Tahar Ben Jelloun mentioned earlier in this chapter shows one way of talking about racism with pupils. Another fine publication is *The Life of Stephen Lawrence* by Verna Allette Wilkins. It is accessible for children from about the age of seven and is of absorbing interest for teenagers. It is beautifully illustrated with full-colour drawings by Lynne Willey, based on family photographs.

Whilst she was still finalising the text the author worked in a number of Oakwell schools as part of the Inspirations, Aspirations project and the book had its official launch at Oakwell Town Hall. Box 51 shows the written comments of some primary school pupils. The first ('heartrending message') was written on the basis of reading material from the book before it was published.

Two reviews by secondary age pupils are shown in Box 52. They make clear that the book has the capacity to engage and stretch teenagers as well as children. Another of the teenage reviewers made a point of quoting the words of Martin Luther King which appear as a kind of frontispiece for the book, before the table of contents: 'Peace is not the absence of tension, but the presence of justice. Without justice there will be no peace.' It is a remarkable achievement by Verna Allette Wilkins, that she succeeds in introducing major political and philosophical ideas and values through the format of a book for young children.

Much of *Equality Stories* has been about the importance of listening to children and young people. Appropriately, it is with the voices of young people that the book now closes.

'I have certainly learnt a lot about racism, ' writes Charlotte-Louise, 'and I hope others learn that it does not matter what colour skin you have, it matters whether you have a good personality or not.'

'I am also black,' says Keziah Joseph, 'and Stephen's story makes me feel worried that someone may act against me and I may be killed. I think the lesson of this story is for the Government to take more action to stop racism happening.'

'The only problem with this story, observes Ben, 'is that it is, and will always remain, unfinished.'

'It left me with a lot to think about,' says Priscilla. 'I hope the same is true for you.'

Box 51

It will be a great book

Heartrending message

This is a book about an innocent man who was brutally stabbed and killed at the hands of six racists.

Stephen Lawrence was an eighteen year old who had a good but short life when he was killed on 22 April 1993. When you stop to think about it, it just makes you feel awful. He was unfairly killed for no reason. The killers have never been found but hopefully they will be some day.

Stephen Lawrence had a lot going for him and could have become a famous person, making a difference to this world. The book describes his tragic death very well. It sends a heartbreaking message and will be a great book.

Duncan, aged 11

Many prejudiced people out there

Stephen Lawrence was a man that had a lot of love from his family and friends. I would never know or feel how his family would feel about his death. The people that stabbed Stephen should be thrown in jail and have the key buried in the ocean. I have certainly learnt a lot about racism and I hope others learn that it does not matter what colour skin you have, it matters whether you have a good personality or not.

What happened to Stephen Lawrence should never happen again. He died at such a young age. I think that the people that stabbed Stephen Lawrence should not take all the blame. A child cannot learn to be racist just like that, it takes the parents to raise the child like that.

I think that the story was wonderful and it showed me that there are still many prejudiced people out there.

Charlotte-Louise, aged 10

The government to take more action

Stephen Lawrence was good at maths, art and architecture. He was also good at running like I am. Unfortunately when he and his friend were standing at the bus stop a gang of Caucasian bullies started calling racist names. Stephen did not have time to run and was stabbed to death by the gang.

I am also black and Stephen's story makes me feel worried that someone may act against me and I may be killed. I think the lesson of this story is for the Government to take more action to stop racism happening. The Prime Minister could appear on television and ask the country why are we killing our black people when we are all the same, just a different colour skin.

I think other people who read this story will feel the same if they are black. If they are not black they should at least tell other white people who feel badly about black people that we are all the same.

Keziah Joseph, aged 8

Box 52

A lot to think about

Like you or me

When I was told about the Stephen Lawrence biography my first thoughts were that it would be a documentation of his brutal and unjust death and the attempts to find his killers. I am very pleased to see it is not that. Instead it is a personal look into the life of Stephen Lawrence from childhood up. For me this brought me closer to him as a person, not a tragic victim and made him more real to me. It made me realise that this was just an ordinary person like you or me, with a bright future that was tragically cut short. I particularly liked the comments from the family friends and teachers who knew him, and stories about his favourite hip-hop and sports stars.

The things that stuck in my mind most when I finished reading the book was not the part about his attack but the stories of his life, especially as a child. As I can identify with them; the stories of his misdemeanours, fights, sibling arguments and fall outs are all more than familiar to me in my own life.

I really like the fact that, in documenting the attack against Stephen, it did not linger on the injustice, nor did it call for action to be taken by the readers. It didn't even document the flaws in the investigation. No, it simply gave you a look into the personal life of Stephen, the facts of his attack, the subsequent investigation and left you to come to your own conclusion. It left me with a lot to think about. I hope the same is true for you.

Priscilla, aged 15

Will always remain unfinished

In response to the yet unpublished biography of Stephen Lawrence that I lately had the privilege of reading, I must say that I was very impressed not only by his character (because it's needless to say that Stephen Lawrence was an extraordinary human being), but by the way in which the book was written so that people of every age group could understand, but on different levels. I feel as a teenager the book wasn't patronising in any way, as it didn't beat about the bush so to speak, as many books do when children are able to access them. It confronts the issue of his death without insulting the reader's intelligence. It also shows that Stephen wasn't perfect, he too had his flaws, but was extremely caring and respectful, as I know of few individuals who run marathons for charity at the age of fourteen.

The only problem with this story is that it is, and will always remain, unfinished, as it is based only on seventeen years of his life and should have had thousands of other moments that should have occurred as Stephen grew older.

In conclusion, *The Life of Stephen Lawrence* is a wonderful story uncovering Stephen's true personality and identity, allowing us to imagine not only his death but his life, which should be celebrated.

Ben, aged 15

7 References and acknowledgements

Chapter 1 – This book's story

The opening quotation from Ben Okri is from his little book *Birds of Heaven*, Phoenix 1996. It is used at the start of Chapter 8 in *The Future of Multi-Ethnic Britain*, Profile Books, 2000.

The inaugural conference at Ealing Town Hall was opened by Alan Parker, the director of education.

'Reflective practitioner': see the reference to Donald Schon in Box 4 and the bibliography.

'IQism': see for example *Rationing Education: policy, reform and equity* by David Gillborn and Deborah Youdell, Open University Press, 2000. There is further discussion in Chapter 4.

Three core values: for further discussion see *The Future of Multi-Ethnic Britain*, Profile Books 2000, particularly the preface and Chapter 4.

'Recognition': a valuable introduction to Charles Taylor's ideas is provided by *Multiculturalism and the Politics of Recognition*, co-authored with Amy Guttman, 1994.

Chapter 2 – How workshops work

Box 4: the authors mentioned here are included in the bibliography. With regard to Freire's theories, see also the book in the bibliography by McClaren and Leonard. The NUT racism awareness training programme in the 1980s was organised by Shirley Darlington. The principal trainers included Terry Mortimer and John Twitchin.

Box 7: each of these quotations appears at the start of a chapter in *The Future of Multi-Ethnic Britain* and acts as an introduction to the chapter's themes.

Box 14: the suggestion that the word 'action' is a useful memorising device was made by tutors at Bradford College and was based on Robin Richardson's earlier idea of 'agenda' in *Daring to be a Teacher*, chapter 10.

Chapter 3 – Listening, welcome and inclusion

Box 15: *Educating Somali Children in Britain* by Mohamed H Kahin, published by Trentham Books, is a valuable handbook to assist teachers respond to the needs of Somali children in their schools. Other useful materials include *Somalis in London*, a report prepared by Leila Hassan Farah and Matthew Smith (Bow Family Centre, Paton Close, Fairfield Road, London E3 2QD); *Brava: an educational resource pack for parents, teachers and other professionals working with the Somali Bravanese Community in the UK*, compiled by Bill Bolloten and Tim Spafford (London Borough of Newham); *Cosob's Journey* by Cosob Mohamed, published by Mantra; *Voices from Somalia* edited by Rachel Warner for the Minority Rights Group; and a range of publications from the Somali publishing house Haan Associates at www.haanbooks.co.uk.

Box 19: the consultant who arranged the visit and subsequently worked with the school was Stuart Scott, director of the Collaborative Learning Project and the Intercultural Education Partnership. There is a wealth of practical teaching ideas at www.collaborativelearning.org.uk

Box 21: the consultant who helped schools to compile this material was Elaine Mace. On English as an additional language more generally, see the books in the bibliography by Brent Language Service, Norah McWilliam and Terry Wrigley, all published by Trentham. With particular regard to bilingualism in early years settings see the book by Charmian Kenner.

Chapter 4 – Great expectations

Lorna Sage: the quotation is from page 21 of *Bad Blood*.

Lee Jasper: from an article in *The Guardian*, 29 May 2001.

Self-fulfilling prophecies: see the book by Robert Tauber in the bibliography.

Howard Gardner's ground-breaking book was *Frames of Mind* (1983). More recently he has published *Intelligence Reframed: multiple intelligences for the 21st century* (1999) and *The Unschooled Mind: how children think and how schools should teach* (1993). Daniel Goleman's best-selling *Emotional Intelligence* has many implications for education. There is discussion of his theories and their application to education in *Defying Disaffection* by Reva Klein.

Accelerated learning: see in particular the handbook by Alistair Smith in the bibliography and the websites of the Accelerated Learning Network at www.accelerated-learning-uk.co.uk and of the Network Educational Press at www.networkpress.co.uk.

Triage: for fuller discussion see Gillborn and Youdell in the bibliography.

Ralph Ellison: the quotation from *Invisible Man* is used by Maud Blair in her study of exclusion entitled *Why Pick On Me?*

Box 30: the quotation is from page 17 of Younge's *No Place Like Home*.

Chapter 5 – We all have a story to tell

Political Quarterly: the editorial was by Andrew Gamble and Tony Wright.

Box 33: the quotation is from page 17 of Simon Schama's book.

Box 34: derived from *The Isles* by Norman Davies. See also *The Future of Multi-Ethnic Britain*, chapter 2. The latter provoked some furious reactions in the media and there is a full account of this at www.runnymedetrust. org/meb.

Box 35: there is an interesting and informative discussion of John Major's speech in *The English* by Jeremy Paxman, Michael Joseph 1998. Mr Major told Paxman that he had been using poetry, and did not expect to be taken literally. See pages 142-44 of Paxman's book and the ensuing discussion of images of Britain and England. Other relevant books include *The Isles* by Norman Davies, (see in particular chapter 10), and *The Future of Multi-Ethnic Britain*, (in particular chapters 1-4). The quotation from Betjeman appears in Paxman's book.

Benjamin Zephaniah's *We Are Britain* is an outstanding introduction for children and young people to the themes of this chapter. There is information at www.benjaminzephaniah. com.

'I believe in Islamophobia': the journalist was Peregrine Worsthorne. There is fuller discussion of the eight features of Islamophobia at www.runnymedetrust.org/meb. (Click on 'Islamophobia' when you get to the home page.)

Box 39: derived from the *Curriculum 2000* documents issued in November 1999 by the Department for Education and Employment and the Qualifications and Curriculum Authority.

Valuable websites for citizenship education include those of the Development Education Centre in Birmingham, www.tidec.org.uk; the Centre for Citizenship Studies in Education at the University of Leicester, www.globaldimension.org.uk; and the Britkids site, impressively re-designed and organized in 2002 at www.britkid.org/ Useful books include *Citizens by Right* by Reva Klein and *Not Aliens* by Hilary Claire.

Chapter 6 – Dealing with racisms

Gary Younge: the quotation is from pages 21-22 of *No Place Like Home*.

Box 43: the definition of racism adapted from the work of the Corrymeela Community originally applied to sectarianism.

Box 46 and Figure 2: the Home Office research was carried out by Rae Sibbitt.

Box 48: adapted slightly from *Preventing and Addressing Racism*, London Borough of Ealing, 2002. Similarly most of the material under the heading of recording and reporting is from this document. For further discussion of these issues see *Toolkit for Tackling Racism* by Stella Dadzie.

Box 49: the model policy statement was compiled in accordance with the *Code of Practice on the Duty to Promote Race Equality* issued by the Commission for Racial Equality in December 2001, and *Preparing a race equality policy for schools*, issued in March 2002. The CRE's handbook *Learning for All* is also a helpful guide. There is full information about these publications on the CRE's website at www.cre.gov.uk.

In addition, as explained in the text of Chapter 6, the model reflects concerns and concepts in *The Future of Multi-Ethnic Britain* and *The Stephen Lawrence Inquiry*. Both these argued that the promotion of race equality necessarily involves also the recognition of cultural diversity. A version of the model was published by the Uniting Britain Trust and the journal *Multicultural Teaching* and can be downloaded from www.runnymedetrust.org/meb. (Click on 'materials for schools' on the home page.)

The whole of the Stephen Lawrence Inquiry report is at http://www.official-documents.co.uk/document/cm42/4262/sli-06.htm. The section dealing with institutional racism is Chapter 6 and is well worth downloading, printing and studying. There is also much valuable material about the Stephen Lawrence Inquiry on the *Guardian* site, www.guardian.co.uk/race, and on the site of the 1990 Trust, www.blink.org.uk.

Bibliography

Ben-Jalloun, Tahar (1999) *Racism Explained to My Daughter.* New York: The New Press

Blair, Maud (2001) *Why Pick On Me? – school exclusion and black youth*, Stoke-on-Trent: Trentham Books

Blair, Maud and Jill Bourne *et al* (1988) *Making the Difference: teaching and learning strategies in successful multi-ethnic schools*, London: Department for Education and Employment

Brent Language Service (1999) *Enriching Literacy: text, talk and tales in today's classroom*, Stoke-on-Trent: Trentham Books

Claire, Hilary (2001) *Not Aliens: primary school children and the citizenship/PSHE curriculum*, Stoke-on-Trent: Trentham Books

Commission for Racial Equality (1999) *Learning for All: standards for racial equality in schools*

Commission on the Future of Multi-Ethnic Britain (2000) *The Future of Multi-Ethnic Britain*, London: Profile Books for the Runnymede Trust

Dadzie, Stella (2000) *Toolkit for Tackling Racism*, Trentham Books

Davies, Norman (1999) *The Isles*, London: Macmillan

Department for Education and Employment (2000) *Removing the Barriers: raising achievement levels for minority ethnic pupils.* DfEE Publications, reference number 0012/2000.

Dunford, John (2001) Making Pupils Behave, *The Guardian*, 12 February.

Gardner, Howard (1999) *Intelligence Reframed: multiple intelligences for the 21st century*, London and New York: Basic Books.

Gardner, Howard (1983) *Frames of Mind*, London and New York: Basic Books

Gillborn, David and Deborah Youdell (2000) *Rationing Education: policy, reform and equity*, Buckingham: Open University Press

Guttman, Amy and Charles Taylor (1994) *Multiculturalism and the Politics of Recognition*, Princeton University Press

Home Office (2001), *Race Relations (Amendment) Act 2000: new laws for a successful multi-racial Britain*, Home Office Communication Directorate.

Jasper, Lee (2201) Brickbats for Oldham, *The Guardian*, 29 May

Kahin, Mohamed (1997) *Educating Somali Children in Britain*, Stoke-on-Trent: Trentham Books

Katz, Judith (1978) *White Awareness: a handbook for antiracism training*, University of Oklahoma Press

Kenner, Charmian (2000) *Home Pages: literacy links for bilingual children*, Stoke-on-Trent: Trentham Books

Klein, Reva (2001) *Citizens by Right: citizenship education in primary schools*, Stoke-on-Trent: Trentham Books for Save the Children

Klein, Reva (1999) *Defying Disaffection: how schools are winning the hearts and minds of reluctant students*, Stoke-on-Trent: Trentham Books

Kolb, David (1983) *Experiential Learning: experience the source of learning development*, New York: Prentice Hall

Lewin, Kurt (1997) *Resolving Social Conflicts and Field Theory in Social Science*, Washington DC: American Psychological Association

Macpherson, William *et al* (1999) *The Stephen Lawrence Inquiry Report.* The Stationery Office. Available on line at www.officialdocuments.co.uk.

McLaren, Peter and Peter Leonard (1993) *Paulo Freire: a critical encounter*, London: Routledge

McWilliam, Norah (1998) *What's in a Word? – vocabulary development in multilingual classrooms*, Stoke-on-Trent: Trentham Books

Office for Standards in Education (2000) *Evaluating Educational Inclusion: guidance for inspectors and schools.* OFSTED.

Paxman, Jeremy (1999) *The English*, London: Penguin Books

Richardson, Robin and Wood, Angela (1999) *Inclusive Schools, Inclusive Society: race and identity on the agenda.* Stoke-on-Trent: Trentham Books

Sage, Lorna (2000) *Bad Blood*, London: Fourth Estate

Schama, Simon (2000) *A History of Britain*, London: BBC Publications

Schon, Donald (1984) *The Reflective Practitioner*, New York and London: Basic Books

Sewell, Tony (2002) *Learning to Succeed*, Birmingham: National Association of Schoolmasters and Union of Women Teachers

Sibbitt, Rae (1997) *The Perpetrators of Racial Harassment and Racial Violence*, London: Home Office Research Study 176

Smith, Alistair (1997) *Accelerated Learning in the Classroom*, Stafford: Network Educational Press

Tauber, Robert (1997) *Self-Fulfilling Prophecy: a practical guide to its use in education*, New York: Praeger Press

Toynbee, Polly (2000) We can be English without Falling into the Racist Trap, *The Guardian*, 12 January

Wilkins, Verna Allette (2001) *The Life of Stephen Lawrence*, London: Tamarind Books

Wrigley, Terry (2000) *The Power to Learn: stories of success in the education of Asian and other bilingual pupils.* Stoke-on-Trent: Trentham Books

Younge, Gary (2000) *No Place Like Home*, London: Picador

Zephaniah, Benjamin (2002) *We Are Britain*, London: Frances Lincoln